SpringerBriefs on Cyber Security Systems and Networks

Editor-in-Chief

Yang Xiang, Digital Research & Innovation Capability Platform, Swinburne University of Technology Digital Research & Innovation Capability, Hawthorn, VIC, Australia

Series Editors

Liqun Chen⊙, Department of Computer Science, University of Surrey Department of Computer Science, Guildford, Surrey, UK

Kim-Kwang Raymond Choo⊙, Department of Information Systems, University of Texas at San Antonio, San Antonio, TX, USA

Sherman S. M. Chow⊙, Department of Information Engineering, the Chinese University of Hong Kong Department of Information Engineering, Hong Kong, Hong Kong

Robert H. Deng⊙, School of Information Systems, Singapore Management University School of Information Systems, Singapore, Singapur, Singapore

Dieter Gollmann, E-15, TU Hamburg-Harburg E-15, Hamburg, Hamburg, Germany

Kuan-Ching Li, Department of Computer Science & Information Engineering, Providence University, Taichung, Taiwan

Javier Lopez, Computer Science Dept., University of Malaga Computer Science Dept., Malaga, Spain

Kui Ren, University at Buffalo null, Buffalo, NY, USA

Jianying Zhou⊙, Infocomm Security Dept, Inst for Infocomm Research Infocomm Security Dept, Singapore, Singapore

The series aims to develop and disseminate an understanding of innovations, paradigms, techniques, and technologies in the contexts of cyber security systems and networks related research and studies.

It publishes thorough and cohesive overviews of state-of-the-art topics in cyber security, as well as sophisticated techniques, original research presentations and in-depth case studies in cyber systems and networks. The series also provides a single point of coverage of advanced and timely emerging topics as well as a forum for core concepts that may not have reached a level of maturity to warrant a comprehensive textbook.

It addresses security, privacy, availability, and dependability issues for cyber systems and networks, and welcomes emerging technologies, such as artificial intelligence, cloud computing, cyber physical systems, and big data analytics related to cyber security research. The mainly focuses on the following research topics:

Fundamentals and theories

- Cryptography for cyber security
- Theories of cyber security
- Provable security

Cyber Systems and Networks

- Cyber systems security
- Network security
- Security services
- Social networks security and privacy
- Cyber attacks and defense
- Data-driven cyber security
- Trusted computing and systems

Applications and others

- Hardware and device security
- Cyber application security
- Human and social aspects of cyber security

More information about this series at http://www.springer.com/series/15797

Chandra Sekhar Mukherjee ·
Dibyendu Roy · Subhamoy Maitra

Design and Cryptanalysis of ZUC

A Stream Cipher in Mobile Telephony

 Springer

Chandra Sekhar Mukherjee
Indian Statistical Institute
Kolkata, West Bengal, India

Dibyendu Roy
Indian Statistical Institute
Kolkata, West Bengal, India

Subhamoy Maitra
Applied Statistics Unit
Indian Statistical Institute
Kolkata, West Bengal, India

ISSN 2522-5561   ISSN 2522-557X   (electronic)
SpringerBriefs on Cyber Security Systems and Networks
ISBN 978-981-33-4881-3   ISBN 978-981-33-4882-0   (eBook)
https://doi.org/10.1007/978-981-33-4882-0

This Springer imprint is published by the registered company Springer Nature Singapore Pte Ltd.
The registered company address is: 152 Beach Road, #21-01/04 Gateway East, Singapore 189721, Singapore

To grown-ups,
who plan to learn cryptology as science.

Foreword

I am delighted to introduce the first complete book on ZUC, one of the recent and widely deployed stream ciphers in Mobile Telephony. Needless to mention that cryptology as a subject is now completely matured. There are a number of excellent books in the domain of general cryptology, or in the well-studied areas like public key cryptosystem or block cipher design and analysis. While there are outstanding research papers regularly appearing in design and analysis of stream ciphers, we still have a dearth of good monographs in this field. In this backdrop, I warmly welcome a dedicated book on the ZUC stream cipher.

This brief document of around a hundred pages has nicely assimilated all the results to make it a complete treatise on ZUC. This cipher is used to encrypt a good proportion of traffic in mobile communication and is believed to be widely used in China. The present book not only explains this stream cipher but also describes where it is placed in the broad spectrum of mobile telephony. Thus, I believe this book will be widely accepted as an important independent monograph for theory and practice in the domain of cryptology. Both students and experienced researchers should benefit from this book.

The book is written by three authors. Chandra Sekhar is presently an M. Tech. (Computer Science) student, Dibyendu is a postdoctoral research fellow and Subhamoy is a senior professor at the Indian Statistical Institute, Kolkata. That is why, this book has a fair blend of student's view, researcher's analysis and teacher's explanation toward understanding a rather advanced subject in a simpler way. I sincerely wish this book will attract serious attention in the domain of Cryptology, Security and Communication as a whole.

Kolkata, India   Bimal Roy
March 2020   Padmasree Awardee
Professor, Indian Statistical Institute
Head, R C Bose Centre for Cryptology and Security
Chairman, National Statistical Commission, India
Founder & Secretary, Cryptology Research Society of India
Former Director, Indian Statistical Institute

Preface

ZUC is a stream cipher which is used to encrypt communications in mobile networks. The basic idea of a stream cipher is simple. This is actually a methodology, where an initial seed will be provided and, in turn, it will generate a stream of data which looks random. However, this is not truly random as the same seed will always generate the same stream if the algorithm is deterministic and the machine is classical. This stream is mixed with plaintext for encryption. The encrypted text is communicated through an open channel with the understanding that no unauthorized third party will be able to decrypt it. On the other hand, the receiver will have the same secret key (the seed) and thus (s)he will be able to generate the same keystream. Then re-mixing the stream and the ciphertext, the plaintext will be recovered. That is, one may immediately understand that the cryptographic security of the whole system primarily depends on the secrecy of the seed (secret key). However, if the stream cipher is not designed properly, or if the complete protocol of data transfer is not properly evaluated, then there may be other problems that might compromise the security. Thus, we have to take care of two issues. One, the proper design of stream cipher, and two, a detailed evaluation of the complete protocol. In this book, we take care of both the issues. While we look at the cipher from cryptographic point of view (more mathematical), at the same time, we present how the stream cipher is placed in the infrastructure of mobile telephony (less mathematical, but an architectural point of view).

ZUC is a stream cipher proposed and designed by China, but it must be mentioned that the cipher was evaluated publicly in the international domain. The design of this cipher was initiated in the first decade of this millennium. In fact, the third author of this book (Subhamoy Maitra) was invited to the first International Workshop on ZUC algorithm during December 2–3, 2010, Beijing, China. Since then, the cipher has experienced several evaluations, certain weaknesses have been identified and the present version, ZUC 1.6 with 128-bit secret key, is believed to be secure. However, being one of the ciphers used in the commercial domain of mobile telephony, it attracts continuous evaluation of the cryptologic community. This should be mentioned that the term 'cryptanalysis' does not mean a complete break of a cipher without knowing the secret key. Cryptanalysis means the detailed evaluation of the cipher using cryptologic techniques. In this book, we explain all the known cryptanalytic results on this cipher.

For analyzing the cipher, we primarily need substantial mathematical background. This is presented in the first introductory chapter. The second chapter is less mathematical, that discusses the mobile telephony architecture and where exactly ZUC is placed in that hierarchy. The experts in the domain of Cryptology and Security may selectively skip the materials of the first two chapters. Chapter 3 provides complete mathematical design and software implementation details (using C programming language) of the ZUC stream cipher. This is the core description of the cipher, that needs to be studied deeply to understand the strength and weaknesses of ZUC. Needless to mention, that the present version ZUC 1.6 does not have any weakness known so far in the public domain. This chapter also discusses how, based on ZUC, the confidentiality and integrity algorithms are implemented in mobile telephony standards such as 3GPP. The last technical chapter (Chap. 4) provides a detailed analysis in terms of the weaknesses of the stream cipher in the earlier version ZUC 1.4. It is very important to understand the details as the users need to be convinced that the present version is indeed secure and there is no obvious trap-door. We conclude this brief document in Chap. 5 with directions toward the future analysis of this cipher.

The readers of this book should have mathematical knowledge at the undergraduate level. However, the first chapter of this book presents the necessary mathematical background so that engineers with good high school-level knowledge can also access this document. A basic background in computer science is necessary with some hands-on experience in C programming. The book supplements all the mathematical details with implementation using C programs. This book does not expect any formal background on cryptology, though basic knowledge in this domain will indeed be an added advantage. This book is targeted toward students and researchers of any science and engineering discipline, and to engineers and professionals who work in the broad field of communication.

Before proceeding further, let us enumerate what is expected from this book.

- This book is a timely report of state-of-the-art analytical techniques in the domain of stream cipher design and analysis with a specific cipher, namely ZUC, in mind.
- This brief document provides a link between new research results and a brief contextual literature review in the domain of complex LFSR-based stream ciphers.
- This draft presents a snapshot of how stream ciphers are deployed in the mobile telephony architecture, one of the most well-known topics for more than half a century in the domain of computer and communication sciences.
- We provide an in-depth study on design and cryptanalysis of ZUC as well as relevant research results in this field.
- This book is a presentation of core concepts toward design and analysis of stream ciphers that involve a basic understanding of electronic circuits such as LFSRs with abstract mathematical objects such as primitive polynomials over finite fields. At the same time, this draft moves forward to explain a very

complex design of a state-of-the-art commercial stream cipher that is implemented in billions of mobile equipments around the world (mostly in China). The research students as well as professional engineers should understand and be aware of the complete timeline and technical know-how in order to make independent contributions in this domain.

A book contains the name of the authors, but we all know that this is actually assimilation of the continuous effort of many people who are continuously working around. We like to acknowledge our family members, co-researchers and friends in this regard. Without their support, this document could not be prepared. We also like to thank our institute, the Indian Statistical Institute. This is needless to mention how prominent this institute is in academic area. At the same time, the kind of academic independence we enjoy in this institute is un-parallel. In this regard, we must thank the Government of India for continuous support toward our research through different departments and agencies. Finally, all the authors like to acknowledge the project (2016–2021) "Cryptography & Cryptanalysis: How far can we bridge the gap between Classical and Quantum Paradigm", awarded to the third author (Subhamoy Maitra) by the Scientific Research Council of the Department of Atomic Energy (DAE-SRC), the Board of Research in Nuclear Sciences (BRNS). Additionally, we would also like to thank Pranab Chakraborty of Wipro Limited as well as Pinakpani Pal and Manmatha Roy of Indian Statistical Institute for improving the quality of the text with valuable suggestions and comments.

As we have pointed out, the third author of this book (Subhamoy Maitra) was a participant in the first International Workshop on ZUC. He cherishes the two initial slides of that presentation a decade back (credit to Dr. Sourav SenGupta, who was Subhamoy's research student at that point of time).

At that time, it was perceived that Cryptology might be an easier subject to handle than the gamut of mobile telephony.

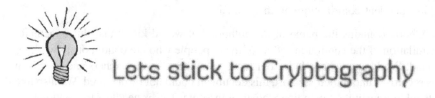

Thus, only cryptology was discussed in the presentation 10 years back. Time flows, and after a decade, we plan to understand the basic framework of mobile telephony too.

We sincerely wish that the readers will enjoy flipping through the pages of this brief document.

Kolkata, India   Chandra Sekhar Mukherjee
March 2020   Dibyendu Roy
                                                                              Subhamoy Maitra

Contents

About the Authors

Chandra Sekhar Mukherjee is currently pursuing M.Tech in Computer Science in Indian Statistical Institute (ISI). He received his B.Tech degree in Computer Science from Heritage Institute of Technology, Kolkata, India in 2019. He was introduced to the field of Cryptology during his internship under the supervision of Prof. Subhamoy Maitra prior to his admission to ISI. The deep connection between probability, combinatorics and number theory that led to the fine line between randomness and bias deeply intrigued him in the domain of Cyptology. Currently his areas of research interest are Cryptology, Quantum Algorithms and Analysis of Boolean Functions. Being in the formative years of his research career, he wishes to contribute in the broad area of secure communication in a meaningful way.

Dr. Dibyendu Roy is a postdoctoral research fellow at the Indian Statistical Institute, Kolkata, India. He obtained his Ph.D. and M.Sc. in Mathematics from the Indian Institute of Technology Kharagpur, India. Earlier, he was a consultant at ERTL (E), STQC, Kolkata, India, and worked in the domain of security analysis. He was also a postdoctoral fellow at the National Institute of Science Education and Research, India, for two years. His primary research area is cryptology, more specifically the domain of symmetric ciphers. His research articles have been published in journals of repute.

Prof. Subhamoy Maitra is Professor at the Indian Statistical Institute (ISI), Kolkata, India. He received his Ph.D. in computer science from the ISI, Kolkata. He holds a M.Tech. in Computer Science from the ISI, Kolkata, and B.Tech. in Electronics and Telecommunications Engineering from Jadavpur University, Kolkata, India. After working briefly in the domain of hardware and software engineering, he joined the ISI, Kolkata, as a faculty in 1997. He has authored several books and around 200 research papers in various fields of cryptology and quantum information.

Notations

0_n	String of zeros of length n.
1_n	String of ones of length n.
$Pr[X]$	Probability of an event X.
$\oplus$	Addition modulo 2 i.e., logical XOR operation.
$\oplus_n$	Bitwise $\oplus$ between two n-bit strings.
$a\|b$	Logical OR operation between a, b.
$\bar{x}$	Complement of x, i.e., $1 \oplus x$.
$\mathbf{0}$	Zero vector.
$\mathbf{x}$	A bit string of certain length.
$a \parallel b$	Concatenation of a and b.
$\#S$, $\|S\|$	The number of elements of a set S.
$\gcd(a,b)$	Greatest common divisor of a, b.
$\|x\|$	Absolute value of an integer x.
$GF(2)$	Field with $\{0, 1\}$, addition and multiplication modulo 2 operation.
$x \lll_n b$	Left rotate by b bits of the n-bit integer x.
$a \gg t$	Right shift of the integer a by t bits.
$a \ll t$	Left shift of the integer a by t bits.
$\boxplus$	Addition modulo 2^{32}.
abc_2	Binary representation of a positive integer.
abc_{16}	Hexadecimal representation of a positive integer.
$\lceil x \rceil$	The smallest integer not less than x.
$x, \tilde{x}$	$x, \tilde{x}$ differ at certain bit/byte positions.
Δx_i	Denotes difference at i-th bit/byte between two bit/byte strings.
$a \equiv b \bmod n$	n divides $(b - a)$
$wt(S)$	Total number of 1's present in a bit string S.
$\mathcal{B}_n$	Set of all n-variable Boolean function.
$L(n)$	Set of all n-variable linear Boolean function.

A_H	Most significant half of bit/byte string A.
A_L	Least significant half of bit/byte string A.
A_{iL}	Least significant i bits of bit string A.
A_{iH}	Most significant i bits of bit string A.

Chapter 1
Introduction and Preliminaries

Abstract In this chapter, we present the introductory materials and mathematical preliminaries that are required for following this material. We describe some basic information regarding ZUC stream cipher and then proceed with the mathematical objects such as finite fields and Boolean functions. These are basic tools in analyzing any building block stream cipher design, such as Linear Feedback Shift Registers. We also explain basic ideas of cryptography and stream ciphers.

Keywords Cryptography · Block cipher · Stream cipher · Boolean function

1.1 Introduction

Cryptography is the scientific art of protecting information in public domain. Any two persons (it is now a well known practice to call them Alice and Bob), who like to exchange information in public channel, but at the same time, are quite concerned to protect their exchanged information from unwanted eavesdropper (Oscar), have to adopt some scientific methodology. In this context, one of the fundamental objectives of cryptography is to transform the confidential information (say plaintext) into an unreadable meaningless format (say ciphertext) in such a way that only the desired person will be able to recover the confidential information (plaintext) from ciphertext. Hence, cryptographic techniques enable Alice and Bob to communicate securely over an insecure channel which is minutely observed by a clever and extremely powerful adversary, Oscar.

The prime objective of exploiting cryptography in our daily life is to achieve either one or all of the following security attributes.

1. **Confidentiality:** This security attribute hides the information from an undesired person. Only a legitimate person will be able to obtain the original plaintext from the publicly available ciphertext.
2. **Integrity:** It is a security feature which allows the receiver to check the correctness of the received message.
3. **Authenticity:** This security feature enables the correctness of the source of the message during communication.

© The Author(s), under exclusive license to Springer Nature Singapore Pte Ltd. 2021   1
C. S. Mukherjee et al., *Design and Cryptanalysis of ZUC*,
SpringerBriefs on Cyber Security Systems and Networks,
https://doi.org/10.1007/978-981-33-4882-0_1

Depending upon the security attributes, different cryptosystems are designed. For confidentiality purpose, cryptosystems are mainly classified into two categories:

1. Symmetric key cryptosystem,
2. Public key cryptosystem.

To provide only confidentiality, a cryptosystem will primarily require two basic functions. The first one, which will convert the plaintext to ciphertext is known as encryption, and the other one which will convert the ciphertext to plaintext is called decryption. An encryption algorithm (Enc) takes a message (M) and an encryption key (e_K) as input to generate corresponding ciphertext (C); i.e., $C = Enc(M, e_K)$. The corresponding decryption function (Dec) will be designed in such a way that it will take the ciphertext C and a decryption key (d_K) as input and recover the original message; i.e., $Dec(C, d_k) = M$.

Depending upon the nature of encryption key and decryption key, classical encryption/decryption algorithms are categorized into two domains. If the encryption key is the same as the decryption key then such an algorithm will be categorized under the Symmetric key cryptosystem. If the encryption key is different from the decryption key then that strategy is placed under the domain of Public key cryptosystem.

1.2 Symmetric Key Cryptosystem

Symmetric encryption–decryption algorithms are based on the main assumption that if a key K is used for encrypting a message then the same key K has to be used during decryption for getting back the correct data. The symmetric key encryption–decryption algorithms are mainly divided into two categories. One is Block cipher and the other, Stream cipher.

In case of a block cipher, first the message M will be divided into multiple blocks of fixed length. Then the encryption of the complete message M will be done by transforming each individual block mixing the secret key. The resulting ciphertext is transmitted from the sender to the receiver.

$$\text{Message} : M = m_0||m_1||\cdots||m_r$$
$$\text{Ciphertext block} : c_i = Enc(m_i, K)$$
$$\text{Ciphertext} : C = c_0||c_1||\cdots||c_r.$$

In the receiving end, to decipher the ciphertext, decryption algorithm needs to be performed block wise.

$$\text{Ciphertext} : C = c_0||c_1||\cdots||c_r$$
$$\text{Message block} : m_i = Dec(c_i, K)$$
$$\text{Message} : M = m_0||m_1||\cdots||m_r.$$

Example of such block ciphers are DES (National Bureau of Standards 1977) and AES (Daemen and Rijmen 2001), which are extremely well referred in cryptology literature.

In case of a stream cipher (Fig. 1.1), encryption/decryption is generally done characterwise (actually bitwise in the lowest level). Here, a random looking sequence of bits of length equal to the message length is generated. This sequence is then bitwise XORed (addition modulo 2) with the message sequence and then the resulting sequence is transmitted. At the receiving end, decryption is done by generating the same random sequence and again bitwise XOR-ing the cipher bits with the random bits. The main advantage of this scheme is that if a fast random bit generator is available, then both encryption and decryption are very fast. The problem however is in the availability of random bit generators. If a truly random generator is used, then of course it is impossible to regenerate the sequence and hence the message cannot be recovered. To get around the problem, one can generate a long sequence of pseudo-random bits and provide both the sender and the receiver with this sequence. When the sender wants to transmit, he uses only a part of the pseudo-random sequence to encrypt. Once used, this part is never used again. Since the communication between the sender and the receiver is synchronous, the receiver uses the correct part of the random sequence from the generator at his end to decrypt the message. Though not practical, such a sequence, if truly random, shared securely and never used again, is called an "one time pad". One Time Pads have the desirable property of perfect secrecy in the information-theoretic sense. One cryptographic scheme is said to be perfectly secure if ciphertext does not reveal any kind of information about plaintext. In mathematical sense, it means $\Pr[M = m | C = c] = \Pr[M = m]$.

Though one time pads offer perfect secrecy, in practice, it is difficult to implement such a scheme, since the distribution of long random bit-stream will require a lot of space. So in practice, one uses a pseudo-random generator at both the sender and receiver ends, set up with the same initial conditions, when they meet physically or share such a key through secure public key algorithms. Thus both the sender and the receiver can generate the same pseudo-random sequence of bits from the same initial seed. In this case, the problem is to get a good pseudo-random generator. Many such generators have been proposed and there are statistical tests to ascertain the pseudo-randomness of a generator. However, for cryptographic purposes, it is important for a generator to be secure. Roughly, this means that given an initial sequence of generated bits $b_0, \ldots, b_k$, it should not be possible to efficiently (in polynomial time) guess the next bit with chances of success significantly greater than half. Such notions have been formalized and different models of cryptographically secure pseudo-random generators have been proposed (Blum et al. 1986).

However, such systems are still not being used for practical purposes due to efficiency issues. In fact, the most popular stream cipher systems are based on Linear Feedback Shift Registers (LFSR) and a Boolean function as in Fig. 1.3. See Golomb (1967) for a detailed discussion on LFSRs. At this point, it is sufficient to consider that LFSRs produce pseudo-random bit sequences with both probability of zero and probability of one equal to half. Thus, we can consider LFSRs as pseudo-random bit

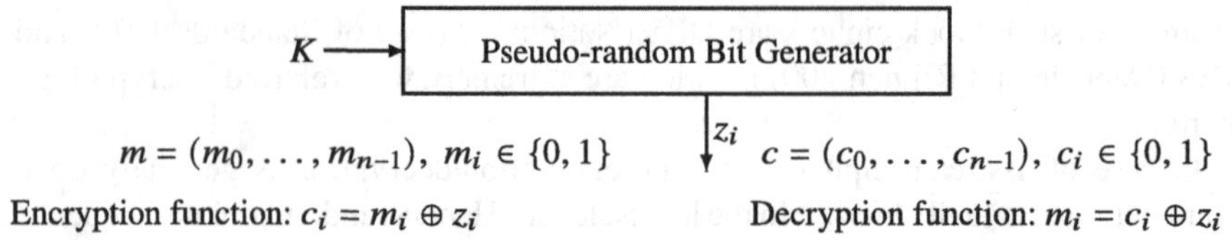

$$K \longrightarrow \boxed{\text{Pseudo-random Bit Generator}}$$

$m = (m_0, \ldots, m_{n-1}), \; m_i \in \{0, 1\}$ $\Big\downarrow z_i$ $c = (c_0, \ldots, c_{n-1}), \; c_i \in \{0, 1\}$

Encryption function: $c_i = m_i \oplus z_i$ Decryption function: $m_i = c_i \oplus z_i$

Fig. 1.1 Stream cipher

generators and the secret key is the initial conditions of the LFSRs, i.e., the seed of the pseudo-random bit generators.

Before getting more into the actual design, let us go through certain prerequisites that will help to understand such cryptographic schemes better.

1.3   Prerequisites

In this section, we describe some basic terminologies and definitions which are used throughout the book. This book mainly focuses on the stream cipher ZUC (design description can be found in Chap. 4), which is based on LFSR. To describe the properties of an LSFR-based stream cipher, we need to build up the certain mathematical background. For this, we start with the basics of finite fields.

1.3.1   Finite Fields

Finite fields play a very crucial role in designing hardware-based stream ciphers. The elements of a field are exploited as characters in LFSRs and are also used to form transformation functions with dedicated properties, among other uses. In this section, we will understand the basic properties of finite fields and how they are used in stream cipher algorithms.

A field is a nonempty set F together with two binary operations $+$ (Addition) and $\cdot$ (multiplication). A field $(F, +, \cdot)$ must satisfy the following properties:

1. $(F, +)$ is a commutative group.
2. If 0 denotes the identity element of the group $(F, +)$, then $(F \setminus \{0\}, \cdot)$ is a commutative group. Here, 0 is denoted as the zero elements of F.
3. For all $a, b, c \in F$, $a \cdot (b + c) = a \cdot b + a \cdot c$.

The set $F \setminus \{0\}$ is also denoted as F^* and $(F^*, \cdot)$ is called the multiplicative group of field $(F, +, \cdot)$. The identity element of F^* is denoted as 1. Every element in F has an additive inverse as $(F, +)$ is a group. Every element except 0 has a multiplicative inverse as $(F^*, \cdot)$ is also a group. The additive inverse of $a \in F$ is denoted as $-a$, while the multiplicative inverse is denoted as a^{-1}. Some examples of fields are $\mathbb{Q}$

(the set of rational numbers with the usual addition and multiplication operator) and $\mathbb{R}$ (the set of real numbers). Here, the sets are not finite.

A field with a finite number of elements is called a finite field. If the complete multiplicative group $(F^*, \cdot)$ can be generated by an element of F^*, then $(F^*, \cdot)$ is known as cyclic group and the element which generates F^* is called a primitive element of F^*.

1.3.1.1 Prime Fields

Modular arithmetic gives us a very nice way to construct finite fields. As we know, in modular arithmetic, an integer $p > 0$ is chosen, and the operations addition $(+)$ and multiplication $(\cdot)$ are performed modulo p. It is interesting to see that the set of remainders of all natural numbers, when taken modulo p, create nice structures with addition and multiplication under the same modulo operation.

Consider a prime number p and the set $\mathbb{F}_p = \{0, 1, \ldots, p-1\}$ with two binary operations standard $+$ and $\cdot$ under modulo p, i.e., for any $x, y \in \mathbb{F}_p$, addition: $z_1 = (x + y) \mod p$, multiplication: $z_2 = x \cdot y \mod p$. One can easily check that $(\mathbb{F}_p, +)$ is a commutative group. To show $(\mathbb{F}_p^*, \cdot)$ is a commutative group under multiplication, we need to show that, for every $a \in \mathbb{F}_p^*$, there exists an unique b such that $a \cdot b \equiv 1 \mod p$. Since p is a prime number, for any $a \in \mathbb{F}_p^*$, $gcd(a, p) = 1$. Therefore, there exists b and r such that $ab + rp = 1$ (example: $gcd(3, 5) = 1$, for this, we have $2 \cdot 3 + (-1) \cdot 5 = 1$). This implies $ab \equiv 1 \mod p$. Hence, for any $a \in \mathbb{F}_p^*$, there exists $b \in \mathbb{F}_p^*$ such that $ab \equiv 1 \mod p$. Now, for this $a \in \mathbb{F}_p^*$, if we consider $\{1 \cdot a, 2 \cdot a, \ldots, (p-1) \cdot a\}$ under modulo p, then there does not exist $i \neq j$, such that $i \cdot a \equiv j \cdot a \mod p$ happens. If it happens then p divides either of $a, (i-j)$. As p is a prime number so it is never possible. This shows the uniqueness of $b \in \mathbb{F}_p^*$ such that $a \cdot b \equiv 1 \mod p$. The rest of the requirements for $(\mathbb{F}_p, +, \cdot)$ to be a field follow trivially. This field is often called the Galois field and is denoted by $GF(p)$.

We state the following property which is required for our discussion. For better understanding, one may refer to Lidl and Niederreiter (1994).

Property 1.1 *If two finite fields* $(F_1, +, \cdot)$ *and* $(F_2, +, \cdot)$ *have the same number of elements, then they are isomorphic.*

Because of this uniqueness, the modulus structure can be used to explain the structure of any finite field of form $GF(p)$, where p is a prime number.

Property 1.2 *The cardinality of any finite field is* p^n, *where* p *is a prime number and* $n \in \mathbb{N}$.

These two properties will be used in the next section.

1.3.2   Field Extension

Here, we discuss the extension of a field. Suppose $(F_1, +, \cdot)$ is a field and $F_2 \subseteq F_1$ is closed under addition $+$ and multiplication $\cdot$. If $(F_2, +, \cdot)$ is also a field then F_2 is known as a subfield of F_1, and F_1 is called field extension of F_2. For example, $\mathbb{Q}$ is a subfield of $\mathbb{R}$ and $\mathbb{R}$ is a field extension of $\mathbb{Q}$.

Polynomials Over a Field. Polynomials can be used to describe and realize elements of a finite field. First, we understand how these polynomials are defined. We consider the polynomials defined over $GF(p) = \{0, 1, \ldots, p - 1\}$, that is all the coefficients of the polynomial belong to $GF(p)$. A polynomial $f(x)$ over $GF(p)$ could therefore be expressed as $f(x) = c_0 + c_1 x + c_2 x^2 + \cdots c_m x^m$, where $c_i \in GF(p), 0 \leq i \leq$, $c_m \neq 0$. Here, m is defined to be the degree of $f(x)$. This can be also be inferred as defining for all $i > m, c_i = 0$.

Now if one considers the field $GF(2) = \{0, 1\}$, with standard addition and multiplication modulo 2 as two binary operations, then the structure of $GF(2)[x]$ will be,

$$GF(2)[x] = \left\{ f \mid f = \sum_i c_1 x^i, \ c_i \in \{0, 1\} \right\}.$$

It is important to understand that two polynomials are differentiated on the basis of the coefficients and not the values obtained by $f(a)$ for all possible values of a and determining if they are similar or dissimilar. For example, in $GF(2)$, both $x + 1$ and $x^2 + 1$ have the same value for both $x = 0$ and $x = 1$. However, they are different polynomials nonetheless. The polynomial arithmetic is fairly simple, and the value of the coefficients are operated on by addition and multiplication modulo p. Now let us define the addition and the multiplication of two polynomials.

Addition and Multiplication of Polynomials. Suppose there are two polynomials $f(x)$ and $g(x)$ defined over $GF(p)$ with $deg(f) = m_1$ and $deg(g) = m_2$ such that $m_1 > m_2$. Given $f(x) = \sum_{i=0}^{m_1} f_i x^i$ and $g(x) = \sum_{i=0}^{m_2} g_i x^i$, the sum of the polynomials is as follows:

$$f(x) + g(x) = \sum_{i=0}^{m_2} ((f_i + g_i) \mod p) x^i + \sum_{j=m_2+1}^{m_1} f_j x^j.$$

That is, addition, and similarly subtraction is done component wise. Multiplication of two polynomials $f(x)$ and $g(x)$ is as follows. Suppose $h(x) = f(x) \cdot g(x)$ with the polynomials f and g as described above. Then the multiplication $h(x) = (\sum_{i=0}^{m_1} f_i x^i) \cdot (\sum_{i=0}^{m_2} g_i x^i)$ will be of degree $m_1 + m_2$. If $h(x) = \sum_{i=0}^{m_1+m_2} h_i x^i$ then

$$h_i = \sum_{j=0}^{i} f_j \cdot g_{i-j} \mod p.$$

The set of all polynomials with coefficients from a field F is denoted as $F[x]$. The set $F[x]$ under addition (+) forms an abelian group with the zero-polynomial as the identity element. It is also closed under multiplication (denoted by ·) and is associative in nature. The polynomial $1 \in F[x]$ is the multiplicative identity. However, all the polynomials might not have a multiplicative inverse and therefore $(F[x], +, \cdot)$ form a ring and not a field.

Suppose $F[x]$ be a polynomial ring over a field F. A polynomial $p(x) \in F[x]$ with $deg(p(x)) \geq 1$ will be called an irreducible polynomial if $p(x)$ cannot be expressed as $p_1(x) \cdot p_2(x)$, where $p_1(x), p_2(x) \in F[x]$ with degree ≥ 1. Suppose $p(x) \in F[x]$ be an irreducible polynomial and $I = \langle p(x) \rangle = \{p(x) \cdot q(x) | q(x) \in F[x]\}$. It can be proven that $F[x]/I$ will become a field. (We leave the prove as an exercise for the readers.) The zero element of $F[x]/I$ is the zero polynomial. Now if the degree of $p(x)$ is n, then the field $F[x]/\langle p(x) \rangle$ will be

$$F[x]/\langle p(x) \rangle = \{a_0 + a_1 x + \cdots + a_{n-1} x^{n-1} | a_0, a_1, \ldots, a_{n-1} \in F\}.$$

Hence, $F[x]/\langle p(x) \rangle$ will contain $|F|^n$ elements. Here, the addition of two polynomials $p_1, p_2 \in F[x]/\langle p(x) \rangle$ will be performed as follows,

$$(a_0 + a_1 x + \cdots + a_{n-1} x^{n-1}) + (b_0 + b_1 x + \cdots + b_{n-1} x^{n-1})$$
$$= (a_0 + b_0) + (a_1 + b_1)x + \cdots + (a_{n-1} + b_{n-1})x^{n-1},$$

where $(a_i + b_i)$ is performed under the field operation in F and $p_1 = a_0 + a_1 x + \cdots + a_{n-1} x^{n-1})$, $p_2(x) = (b_0 + b_1 x + \cdots + b_{n-1} x^{n-1})$. Similarly, the multiplication between $p_1(x), p_2(x) \in F[x]/\langle p(x) \rangle$ is performed as follows:

1. First find $p_1(x) \cdot p_2(x) \in F[x]$,
2. Divide $p_1(x) \cdot p_2(x)$ by $p(x)$ and find the remainder $r(x)$.

This $r(x)$ will be the multiplication result of $p_1(x)$ and $p_2(x)$ in $F[x]/\langle p(x) \rangle$. By following the same procedure, one can find inverse of any $g(x) \in F[x]/\langle p(x) \rangle \setminus \{0\}$.

Now one can easily check that $\{a | a \in F\}$ is a subset of $F[x]$. In fact, $\{a | a \in F\}$ is a subfield of $F[x]/\langle p(x) \rangle$ which is isomorphic to F, where $p(x)$ is an irreducible polynomial. Hence, $F[x]/\langle p(x) \rangle$ is a field extension of F. It can be observed that all the elements of $F[x]/\langle p(x) \rangle$ are constructed by taking modulo $p(x)$. Hence, all the elements of $F[x]/\langle p(x) \rangle$ can be represented as a polynomial in α, where $p(\alpha) = 0$. We also denote $F[x]/\langle p(x) \rangle$ as $F[\alpha]$, where α is a formal root of $p(x) \in F[x]$. Note that α is a formal root of $p(x)$ which does not belong to F as $p(x)$ is an irreducible polynomial over F.

Example 1.1 Let $F = GF(2) = \{0, 1\}$ and $p(x) = x^2 + x + 1 \in GF(2)[x]$. It can be checked that $p(0) \neq 0$ and $p(1) \neq 0$. Hence $p(x)$ is an irreducible polynomial over $GF(2)$. Now we construct an extension field of $GF(2)$ by considering the irreducible polynomial $p(x)$. Let α be a root of $p(x)$, i.e., $p(\alpha) = 0$. So we will have $\alpha^2 = \alpha + 1$. Hence, the elements of the extension field are $0, 1, \alpha, \alpha^2$. As $\alpha^2 = \alpha + 1$, so the final elements of the extension field will be $\{0, 1, \alpha, \alpha + 1\}$.

Suppose $p(x) \in F[x]$ is an irreducible polynomial over F and α be a formal root of $p(x)$, i.e., $p(\alpha) = 0$. If α is a primitive element of the corresponding extension field, then $p(x)$ will be called a primitive polynomial. Here, we consider an example to understand the difference between an irreducible polynomial and a primitive polynomial.

Example 1.2 We consider two polynomials $p_1(x) = x^4 + x^2 + 1 \in GF(2)[x]$, $p_2(x) = x^4 + x + 1 \in GF(2)[x]$, where $GF(2) = \{0, 1\}$. One can easily check that both these polynomials are irreducible polynomials.

Consider the polynomial $p_1(x)$ and the extension field $GF(2)[x]/\langle p_1(x) \rangle$. It can be easily checked that the extension field $GF(2)[x]/\langle p_1(x) \rangle$ will contain 16 elements. Let α be a formal root of $p_1(x)$, hence, $p_1(\alpha) = 0$. With this root α we can compute the following:

$$\alpha^0 = 1, \alpha^1 = \alpha, \alpha^2 = \alpha^2, \alpha^3 = \alpha^3, \alpha^4 = \alpha^2 + 1,$$
$$\alpha^5 = \alpha^3 + \alpha, \alpha^6 = \alpha^4 + \alpha^2 = 1.$$

It can be seen that $\alpha^6 = 1$, so the element α will not be able to generate the complete extension field. Hence, α is not a primitive element of the extension field and $p_1(x)$ is not a primitive polynomial.

Now consider the second polynomial $p_2(x)$. Further consider the extension field $GF(2)[x]/\langle p_2(x) \rangle$. One can check that this extension field also contains 16 elements. Let β be a formal root of $p_2(x)$, hence $p_2(\beta) = 0$. Here, we can compute as follows:

$$\beta^0 = 1, \beta^1 = \beta, \beta^2 = \beta^2, \beta^3 = \beta^3, \beta^4 = \beta + 1, \beta^5 = \beta^2 + \beta, \beta^6 = \beta^3 + \beta^2,$$
$$\beta^7 = \beta^4 + \beta^3 = \beta^3 + \beta + 1, \beta^8 = \beta^4 + \beta^2 + \beta = \beta^2 + 1, \beta^9 = \beta^3 + \beta,$$
$$\beta^{10} = \beta^4 + \beta^2 = \beta^2 + \beta + 1, \beta^{11} = \beta^3 + \beta^2 + \beta,$$
$$\beta^{12} = \beta^4 + \beta^3 + \beta^2 = \beta^3 + \beta^2 + \beta + 1, \beta^{13} = \beta^4 + \beta^3 + \beta^2 + \beta = \beta^3 + \beta^2 + 1,$$
$$\beta^{14} = \beta^4 + \beta^3 + \beta = \beta^3 + 1, \beta^{15} = \beta^4 + \beta = 1.$$

It can be observed that β generates 15 distinct elements. Thus, β is a primitive element of the extension field. Hence, $p_2(x)$ is a primitive polynomial.

We now understand the difference between $GF(p^n)$ and $GF(p^n - 1)$, where p and $p^n - 1$ are prime. Although the sizes of the two fields are very close, their representations are quite different. This is because $GF(p^n)$ is an extension field of $GF(p)$, whereas $GF(p^n - 1)$ is a prime field. This is important to understand as in the later chapters we will see that the LFSR used in ZUC cipher is based on $GF(2^{31} - 1)$, and this property affects the randomness of the cipher. We consider the following example for better understanding.

Example 1.3 We explain $GF(2^2)$ and $GF(2^2 - 1) = GF(3)$ to showcase the differences. Here, $GF(2^2)$ can be realized using a primitive polynomial of degree 2 over $GF(2)$. One such polynomial is $x^2 + x + 1$. We can realize the field using α such that $\alpha^2 + \alpha + 1 = 0$, i.e., $\alpha^2 = \alpha + 1$. Thus, the elements of $GF(2^2)$ are $\{0, 1, \alpha, \alpha + 1\}$. On the other hand, the elements of $GF(3)$ are constructed by taking

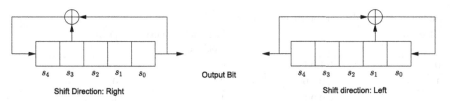

Fig. 1.2 A 4-bit LFSR with left/right-shift mechanism

modulo 3 arithmetic. Hence, the elements of $GF(3)$ can be represented as $\{0, 1, 2\}$. As these elements are generated by taking modulo 3, hence $\{0, 1, 2\}$ and $\{3, 1, 2\}$ are equivalent.

Given that we understand how to realize any field of cardinality p^n (p prime), let us now proceed to the concept of LFSRs and the stream ciphers.

1.3.3 LFSR-Based Stream Cipher

A Linear Feedback Shift Register is a pseudo-random bit (number) generator which is used in many hardware-based stream ciphers such as Grain-v1 (Hell et al. 2020), ZUC (ZUC Specification 2011). An n-bit LFSR is based on an n-bit register and a linear feedback function. The state of the n-bit LFSR must be initialized by an initial n-bit state. In each clocking (round) all the state bits shift in a predetermined direction (either left or right). Due to this, shifting one state bit (either rightmost or leftmost) will go out of the register and one state bit position (either leftmost or rightmost) will become empty. The bit, which is going out from the register, is known as the output bit. The empty position of the state will be set to a bit value, which is known as the feedback bit. The feedback bit is the output of a linear function involving certain state bits of the LFSR prior to the shift. A pictorial representation of a 4-bit LFSR (with left and right shifting) is provided in Fig. 1.2.

Depending on the direction of the shift, LFSR's working principle can be expressed in one of the following two ways. Let the state bits of an n-bit LFSR at tth clock be $s_0^t, s_0^t, \ldots, s_{n-1}^t$. Now if the shift direction of the LFSR is toward right, then we will have the following mathematical modeling of the LFSR.

$$s_i^{t+1} = s_{i+1}^t \text{ for } 0 \leq i < n - 1,$$
$$s_{n-1}^{t+1} = f(s_0^t, s_1^t, \ldots, s_{n-1}^t), \text{ where } f \text{ is a linear function,}$$
$$s_0^t = \text{Output at } (t + 1)\text{th clock.}$$

Similarly, if the shift direction is towards the left, then the mathematical modeling of the LFSR will be,

Table 1.1 State update and output of an LFSR

Clocking	$s_3\ s_2\ s_1\ s_0$	Feedback for next clocking	Output bit
0	0 1 0 1	0	1
1	0 0 1 0	0	0
2	0 0 0 1	1	1
3	1 0 0 0	0	0
4	0 1 0 0	1	0
5	1 0 1 0	0	0
6	0 1 0 1	0	1

$$s_i^{t+1} = s_{i-1}^t \text{ for } 1 \le i < n,$$
$$s_0^t = f(s_0^t, s_1^t, \ldots, s_{n-1}^t) \text{ where } f \text{ is a linear function,}$$
$$s_{n-1}^t = \text{ Output at } (t+1)\text{th clock.}$$

Hence, any LFSR is essentially defined by its shift procedure and the linear feedback function f, which can be expressed as

$$f(s_0, s_1, \ldots, s_{n-1}) = \oplus_{i=0}^{n-1} c_i s_i,$$

where the coefficients $c_i \in \{0, 1\}$, $i = 0, \ldots, n-1$ are constants and $s_i \in \{0, 1\}$, $i = 0, \ldots, n-1$ are the state bits of the LFSR.

Example 1.4 Consider a 4-bit LFSR with right shift mechanism. The state bits of the LFSR is denoted by s_i, $i = 0, \ldots, 3$. The feedback function of the LFSR is,

$$f_1(s_0, s_1, s_2, s_3) = s_0 \oplus s_2.$$

Hence, the 4 coefficients of the feedback function are $c_1 = c_3 = 0$, $c_0 = c_2 = 1$. We first initialize the state bits of the LFSR to certain values. It can be observed that if we initialize all state bits to be zero, then every clocking the feedback bit will also be zero. Hence, the state of the LFSR remain fixed to the initial state (i.e., zero state). So, for all practical purposes, we need to consider a non-zero state. For example, let us initialize the state with $s_0 = s_2 = 1$ and $s_1 = s_3 = 0$. With this, we start the clocking of the LFSR. In Table 1.1, we show the state update and the output in each clock. It can be observed that after 6 clockings, the state of the LFSR becomes identical to the initial state.

Now we consider a different linear feedback function

$$f_2 = s_0 \oplus s_3.$$

Table 1.2 State update and output of an LFSR

Clocking	$s_3\ s_2\ s_1\ s_0$	Feedback for next clocking	Output bit
0	0 1 0 1	1	1
1	1 0 1 0	1	0
2	1 1 0 1	0	1
3	0 1 1 0	0	0
4	0 0 1 1	1	1
5	1 0 0 1	0	1
6	0 1 0 0	0	0
7	0 0 1 0	0	0
8	0 0 0 1	1	1
9	1 0 0 0	1	0
10	1 1 0 0	1	0
11	1 1 1 0	1	0
12	1 1 1 1	0	1
13	0 1 1 1	1	1
14	1 0 1 1	0	1
15	0 1 0 1	1	1

Table 1.3 State update and output of an LFSR

Clocking	$s_3\ s_2\ s_1\ s_0$	Feedback for next clocking	Output bit
0	0 1 0 1	1	1
1	1 0 1 0	0	0
2	0 1 0 1	1	1

For this feedback function, the same initial state $s_0 = s_2 = 1$, $s_1 = s_3 = 0$, will generate different state and output bit. In Table 1.2, we describe the state update and output bit for different clock. In this scenario, after 15 many clockings, the state of the LFSR becomes identical with the initial state.

Now if we consider the feedback function $f_3(s_0, s_1, s_2, s_3) = s_0$ and the same initial state we get the same state after 2 clockings as shown in Table 1.3.

The number of clocking after which the state of an LFSR becomes identical to the initial state is known as the period. In this case, the total number of possible states of the LFSR is 16 (as there are four state bits and each bit can be either 0 or 1). It is worth to note that starting from a non-zero state, it is not possible to reach the zero state if there is a feedback (say $c_0 = 1$). Therefore, in this case (i.e., for 4-bit LFSR), the maximum period of an LFSR can be $2^4 - 1 = 15$. With a similar argument, for an n-bit LFSR, the maximum period will be $2^n - 1$. Let us now see when this happens.

The feedback function of an n-bit LFSR can be seen as an n-degree polynomial over $GF(2)$. That is, the coefficients of this n-degree polynomial belong to $\{0, 1\}$. Suppose the feedback function is $f = \oplus_{i=0}^{n-1} c_i s_i$, where $s_i \in \{0, 1\}, i = 0, \ldots, n-1$ are the state bits and $c_i \in \{0, 1\}, i = 0, \ldots, n-1$ are the constants. This feedback function can be corresponded to a polynomial $g(x)$ of degree n over $GF(2)$, where

$$g(x) = 1 + c_{n-1}x + c_{n-2}x^2 + \cdots + c_0 x^n.$$

This polynomial is known as feedback polynomial of the LFSR. One may also consider the representation that $g'(x) = x^n + c_{n-1}x^{n-1} + c_{n-2}x^{n-2} + \cdots + c_1 x^1 + c_0$. It is easy to see that $g(x)$ and $g'(x)$ are reciprocal to each other.

An n-bit LFSR can take any of the 2^n possible states. These states can be seen as elements of a field $GF(2^n)$ with 2^n elements. In each clocking, the LFSR generates an element (maybe new) of the same field from the current state. If the LFSR has a full period then the LFSR will generate all $2^n - 1$ distinct non-zero elements starting from a specific one (which must be non-zero).

We recall Example 1.4 where we have considered a 4-bit LFSR. The first feedback function, we have considered was $f_1(s_0, s_1, s_2, s_3) = s_0 \oplus s_2$. The 4-degree feedback polynomial corresponding to this linear feedback function f_1 will be,

$$g_1(x) = x^4 + x^2 + 1.$$

The second feedback function, we have considered was $f_2(s_0, s_1, s_2, s_3) = s_0 \oplus s_3$. The 4-degree feedback polynomial corresponding to this linear feedback function f_2 will be,

$$g_2(x) = x^4 + x + 1.$$

The third feedback function considered in the same example was $f_3(s_0, s_1, s_2, s_3) = s_0$. The corresponding feedback polynomial will be,

$$g_3(x) = x^4 + 1.$$

It can be noticed that the period of the LFSR corresponding to the feedback function f_1 is 6 and the period of the LFSR corresponding to the feedback function f_2 is 15. The LFSR with feedback function f_2 has the full period. Now from Example 1.2, one can check that the function $g_1(x)$ is not a primitive polynomial but the polynomial $g_2(x)$ is a primitive polynomial. One can recall that the root of a primitive polynomial is a primitive element of the corresponding extension field. Now if the feedback polynomial corresponding to the linear feedback function of an LFSR is a primitive polynomial of the corresponding extension field then the LFSR will be full periodic. One can note that $g_3(x)$ is a reducible polynomial over $GF(2)$ and the LFSR with feedback function f_3 has period 2. It is obvious that LFSR designed using reducible feedback polynomial will definitely not give full periodicity. Hence, depending upon the choice of feedback function the period of the corresponding LFSR will vary.

To design a good pseudo-random generator based on LSFR, one would like to achieve full periodicity in the output bits. For that, the feedback polynomial corresponding to the linear feedback function must be a primitive polynomial.

Here, we have discussed an LFSR when the register is initialized with a non-zero bit pattern. Depending upon the requirements, one may initialize the state by bytes/words to construct byte/word-oriented stream cipher. One such construction is the ZUC stream cipher, which is described in Chap. 4.

1.4 Nonlinear Combiner and Filter Generator Model

Whenever cryptanalysis of stream cipher is considered, we assume there are plenty of keystream bits available to the adversary corresponding to a particular key. The famous Berlekamp Massey algorithm (Katz et al. 1996, Chap. 6, Sect. 2) shows that one can construct an n-bit LFSR that produces the stream if $2n$ continuous output bits are available. Thus, just using an LFSR as a stream cipher is absolutely not secure. One may also note that an LFSR is essentially reversible. Given n-consecutive output bits of an LFSR, the initial state can be easily discovered.

That is why we concentrate on a model of LFSR based stream cipher with nonlinear Boolean function. We consider a nonlinear Boolean function $f : \{0, 1\}^n \rightarrow \{0, 1\}$ and LFSR(s) with primitive polynomial(s) p as its feedback polynomial. This nonlinear function f is used together with the LFSR(s) to generate the keystream having increased security parameters.

In literature, there are different constructions of LFSR-based stream ciphers using nonlinear Boolean functions. One model considers a single l-bit LFSR and a nonlinear n-variable ($n \le l$) Boolean function f. The function takes n out of l bits and generate one bit keystream at each clock. If $s_0^t, s_1^t, \ldots, s_{l-1}^t$ be the state bits of the LFSR at tth clock, the keystream bit at tth clock is $z_t = f(s_{i_1}^t, s_{i_2}^t, \ldots, s_{i_n}^t)$. Another model of LFSR-based stream cipher considers n many independent LFSRs and an n-bit nonlinear Boolean function f. Each LFSR generates one bit in each clock, and the nonlinear Boolean function combines these output bits and generates keystream bit. If x_j^t is the output from the jth LFSR at tth clock, then the keystream bit at tth clock will be $z_t = f(x_1^t, \ldots, x_n^t)$. The combination of the above two ideas had been studied by Sarkar (2002). This is based on an n-variable Boolean function f and k many LFSRs ($1 < k < n$). The jth LFSR generates l_j many bits at tth clock. Out of these, i_j bits $x_{j,1}^t, \ldots, x_{j,i_j}^t$ are selected and $i_1 + \cdots + i_k = n$. The keystream bit z_t will be $z_t = f(x_{1,1}^t, \ldots, x_{1,i_1}^t, x_{2,1}^t, \ldots, x_{2,i_2}^t, \ldots, x_{k,1}^t, \ldots, x_{k,i_k}^t)$. For any LFSR-based stream cipher models, if the selected Boolean function f is not carefully chosen, then the system becomes susceptible to several kinds of cryptanalytic techniques such as correlation attack, differential attack, algebraic attack, etc. As Boolean function plays an important role in the security of such stream ciphers, we need to learn some cryptographic properties in this regard.

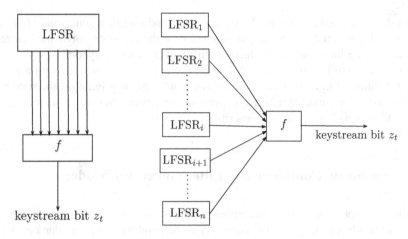

Fig. 1.3 LFSR-based pseudo-random bit generator

1.5 Cryptographic Properties of Boolean Function

An n-variable Boolean function is a mapping from $\{0, 1\}^n$ to $\{0, 1\}$. One can interpret a Boolean function as the output column of the truth table. A truth table contains tabulation of all possible combinations of input values and their corresponding outputs. The Table 1.4 provides an example of a 3-variable Boolean function. The input variables x_3, x_2, x_1 are tabulated in each row. The function is represented in the rightmost column. For an n-variable Boolean function, the truth table contains n columns for inputs, 1 column for output and 2^n rows for all the enumerations of the input variables.

We will generally use the notation $\mathcal{B}_n$ to denote the set of all n-variable Boolean functions. One can easily check that $|\mathcal{B}_n| = 2^{2^n}$.

Table 1.4 Truth table of a 3 variable Boolean function

x_3	x_2	x_1	f
0	0	0	1
0	0	1	1
0	1	0	0
0	1	1	1
1	0	0	1
1	0	1	0
1	1	0	0
1	1	1	0

Definition 1.1 For binary strings S_1, S_2 of same length λ, we denote by #($S_1 = S_2$) (respectively #($S_1 \neq S_2$)), the number of places where S_1 and S_2 are equal (respectively unequal).

The Hamming distance between S_1, S_2 is denoted as $d(S_1, S_2)$, i.e., $d(S_1, S_2) =$ #($S_1 \neq S_2$).

The Walsh Distance is defined as, $wd(S_1, S_2) = $#$(S_1 = S_2) - $#$(S_1 \neq S_2)$. Note that, $wd(S_1, S_2) = \lambda - 2d(S_1, S_2)$.

Also the Hamming weight or simply the weight of a binary string S means the number of 1's in S. This is denoted by $wt(S)$.

Next, we define balancedness.

Definition 1.2 A function $f \in \mathcal{B}_n$ is said to be balanced if its output column in the truth table contains equal number of 0's and 1's (i.e., $wt(f) = 2^{n-1}$).

Note that the combining function in any cryptographic scheme should be balanced. Otherwise, for a large set of randomly selected input values, the proportion of 0's and 1's in the output might be away from half and the system will become vulnerable to cryptanalytic attacks.

Apart from truth table, a Boolean function can also be represented as a multivariate polynomial over $GF(2)$. This representation is known as algebraic normal form (ANF) of that Boolean function. Below we define ANF of an n-variable Boolean function $f(x_1, x_2, \ldots, x_n)$.

$$f(x_1, x_2, \ldots, x_n) = a_0 \oplus \left(\bigoplus_{i=1}^{i=n} a_i x_i\right) \oplus \left(\bigoplus_{1 \leq i \neq j \leq n} a_{ij} x_i x_j\right) \oplus \cdots \oplus a_{12\ldots n} x_1 x_2 \cdots x_n,$$

where the coefficients $a_0, a_{ij}, \ldots, a_{12\ldots n} \in \{0, 1\}$.

Definition 1.3 The number of input variables in the highest order product term with nonzero coefficient is called the algebraic degree, or simply degree.

If the degree of a Boolean function is one then that function is known as affine function. An affine function f can be expressed as $f = \bigoplus_{i=1}^{n} a_i x_i \oplus b$, where $b \in \{0, 1\}$ for all i. We denote the set of all n-variable affine functions by $L(n)$. An affine function with constant term equal to zero is known as linear function. Hence, the ANF of a linear function f will be $f = a_1 x_1 \oplus a_2 x_2 \oplus \cdots \oplus a_n x_n$, where $a_i \in \{0, 1\}$. A Boolean function f of n variables is said to be nonlinear if f is not affine. An affine function with the constant term equals to zero is known as linear function.

Example 1.5 Let us consider a 3-variable nonlinear Boolean function $f = x_0 + x_1 + x_1 x_2$. Here the degree of f is 2.

In the stream cipher model we consider here, the combining function f is so chosen that it increases the linear complexity (Rueppel 1986) of the resulting keystream. High algebraic degree provides high linear complexity (Rueppel and Staffelbach

1987; Ding et al. 1991). The linear complexity of a keystream is the length of the shortest LFSR which is able to generate the same sequence of bits. For secure stream cipher systems, large linear complexity is necessary.

The maximum algebraic degree achievable for an n-variable Boolean function is n. However, such a function is not balanced. The maximum algebraic degree of a balanced function is $n - 1$. Moreover, if a Boolean function possesses the property correlation immunity (which is defined later), then the upper bound on algebraic degree reduces further.

Another important cryptographic property for a Boolean function is high non-linearity. A function with low nonlinearity is prone to Best Affine Approximation (BAA) (Ding et al. 1991, Chap. 3) attack. It is a known plaintext attack and the attack needs the knowledge of the combining function. Best Affine Approximation means approximating the combining function by the closest affine function. Thus, for cryptographic applications, we need functions with high nonlinearity so that they can not be approximated using the affine ones. Below we present the definition of nonlinearity.

Definition 1.4 The measure of nonlinearity of an n variable function f is $nl(f) = \min_{g \in L(n)} (d(f, g))$, i.e., the minimum distance from the set of all n-variable affine functions.

Another important property of an n-variable combiner function f, which combines output from n LFSRs (see Fig. 1.3), is the keystream bit z should not have any statistical dependency with the linear combination of a small subset of the LFSR outputs. If this kind of dependency is present, then this LFSR-based stream cipher will be prone to correlation attack (see Siegenthaler 1985 for more detail). Such correlation attacks can be prevented by using a combiner function with a certain order of correlation immunity (see Siegenthaler 1984). We will define it soon after explaining the Walsh (or Walsh–Hadamard) spectrum of a Boolean function.

Definition 1.5 The Walsh–Hadamard transformation of an n-variable Boolean function f is a mapping from $\{0, 1\}^n$ to $[-2^n, 2^n]$ as defined below,

$$\mathcal{W}_f : \{0, 1\}^n \to [-2^n, 2^n],$$
$$\mathcal{W}_f(\mathbf{a}) = \sum_{\mathbf{x} \in \{0,1\}^n} (-1)^{f(\mathbf{x}) \oplus \mathbf{a} \cdot \mathbf{x}}. \tag{1.1}$$

From the above definition, it can be observed that if f is a balanced Boolean function then $\mathcal{W}_f(\mathbf{0}) = 0$. Equation (1.1) can also be seen in the following direction.

$$\mathcal{W}_f(\mathbf{a}) = \sum_{\mathbf{x} \in \{0,1\}^n} (-1)^{f(\mathbf{x}) \oplus \mathbf{a} \cdot \mathbf{x}}.$$
$$= \left| \mathbf{x} \in \{0, 1\}^n : f(\mathbf{x}) = \mathbf{a} \cdot \mathbf{x} \right| - \left| \mathbf{x} \in \{0, 1\}^n : f(\mathbf{x}) \neq \mathbf{a} \cdot \mathbf{x} \right|.$$

Now, we are in a stage of deriving a relation between $d(f, l_{a,0})$, where $l_{a,0} = \mathbf{a} \cdot \mathbf{x} \in L(n)$, below we derive that.

$$
\begin{aligned}
d(f, l_{a,0}) &= \frac{1}{2} \left\{ \left| \mathbf{x} \in \{0, 1\}^n \ : \ f(\mathbf{x}) = \mathbf{a} \cdot \mathbf{x} \right| + \left| \mathbf{x} \in \{0, 1\}^n \ : \ f(\mathbf{x}) \neq \mathbf{a} \cdot \mathbf{x} \right| \right\} \\
&\quad - \frac{1}{2} \left\{ \left| \mathbf{x} \in \{0, 1\}^n \ : \ f(\mathbf{x}) = \mathbf{a} \cdot \mathbf{x} \right| - \left| \mathbf{x} \in \{0, 1\}^n \ : \ f(\mathbf{x}) \neq \mathbf{a} \cdot \mathbf{x} \right| \right\} \\
&= \frac{1}{2} 2^n - \frac{1}{2} \left| \mathcal{W}_f(\mathbf{a}) \right| \\
&= 2^{n-1} - \frac{1}{2} \left| \mathcal{W}_f(\mathbf{a}) \right|
\end{aligned}
$$

From the above derivation, we have the following relation between nonlinearity of a Boolean function and Walsh–Hadamard transformation of the same Boolean function.

$$
\begin{aligned}
nl(f) &= \min_{l_{a,0} \in L(n)} d(f, l_{a,0}) \\
&= 2^{n-1} - \frac{1}{2} \max_{\mathbf{a} \in \{0,1\}^n} \left| \mathcal{W}_f(\mathbf{a}) \right|.
\end{aligned} \tag{1.2}
$$

In a similar direction, a relation between the correlation immunity and Walsh–Hadamard transform of f has been identified (Guo-Zhen and Massey 1988). For a detailed explanation, one may also have a look at Cusick and Stănică (2017).

Definition 1.6 An n-variable Boolean function f is called correlation immune (respectively resilient) of order m, $1 \leq m \leq n$ (respectively $0 \leq m \leq n$) if and only if $\mathcal{W}_f(\mathbf{a}) = 0$ for all $\mathbf{a} \in \{0, 1\}^n$ with $wt(\mathbf{a}) = m$.

Below, we consider an example for better understanding of these properties.

Example 1.6 Let us consider a 4-variable Boolean function $f = x_1 \oplus x_2 \oplus x_3 x_4$. The degree of this Boolean function is 2. It can also be observed that this function is a balanced Boolean function. The Walsh–Hadamard transform values of this function are $(0, 0, 0, 8, 0, 0, 0, 8, 0, 0, 0, 8, 0, 0, 0, -8)$. It can be observed that $\mathcal{W}_f(\mathbf{0}) = 0$. The nonlinearity of f is 4. The correlation immunity of the same function is 1. It can also be observed that $\mathcal{W}_f(\mathbf{a}) = 0$ for $0 \leq wt(\mathbf{a}) \leq 1$. Thus, this is also a 1-resilient function.

Substitution boxes (S-box) play an important role in the design of a block ciphers as well as in certain types of stream ciphers. An S-box S is a mapping from $\{0, 1\}^n$ to $\{0, 1\}^m$, where $n \geq m$; i.e., $S : \{0, 1\}^n \rightarrow \{0, 1\}^m$. For any S-box $S : \{0, 1\}^n \rightarrow \{0, 1\}^m$, there exists m number of n-variable Boolean functions. These functions are known as coordinate functions of S-box S. Let $f_i, i = 1, \ldots, m$ be the coordinate functions of S.

$$S : \{0, 1\}^n \to \{0, 1\}^m,$$
$$S(\mathbf{x}) = (f_1(\mathbf{x}), f_2(\mathbf{x}), \cdots, f_m(\mathbf{x})).$$

Hence, the cryptographic properties of an S-box must rely on the cryptographic properties of coordinate functions of the S-box. To study cryptographic properties of an S-box, we need to consider any linear combination of the coordinate functions of S-box. The set of all possible linear combinations of coordinate functions of the S-box S will be

$$\{\mathbf{c} \cdot S(\mathbf{x}) : \mathbf{c} \in \{0, 1\}^m\} = \{ \oplus_{i=1}^m c_i f_i : \mathbf{c} = (c_1, \ldots, c_m), c_i \in \{0, 1\}\}.$$

As each $f_i, i = 1, \ldots, m$ are n-variable Boolean functions, so each linear combination $\oplus_{i=1}^m c_i f_i$, $c_i \in \{0, 1\}$ will be an n-variable Boolean function. Below we provide definition of few cryptographic properties of an S-box. The degree, nonlinearity and correlation immunity of an S-box are defined in Definitions 1.7, 1.8, 1.6.

Definition 1.7 Let $S : \{0, 1\}^n \to \{0, 1\}^m$ be an S-box. The coordinate functions of S are $f_i, i = 1, \ldots, m$. The algebraic degree of S is defined as

$$deg(S) = \min_{\mathbf{c} \in \{0,1\}^m} \{deg(\mathbf{c} \cdot S(\mathbf{x})), \ \mathbf{c} \neq \mathbf{0}\},$$

i.e., minimum degree among degrees of all possible linear combinations of coordinate functions and not all coefficients of the linear combination are zero at the same time.

Definition 1.8 Let $S : \{0, 1\}^n \to \{0, 1\}^m$ be an S-box. The coordinate functions of S are $f_i, i = 1, \ldots, m$. The nonlinearity of S is defined by

$$nl(S) = \min_{\mathbf{c} \in \{0,1\}^m} \{nl(\mathbf{c} \cdot S(\mathbf{x})), \ \mathbf{c} \neq \mathbf{0}\},$$

i.e., minimum nonlinearity among nonlinearities of all possible linear combinations of coordinate functions and not all coefficients of the linear combination are zero at the same time.

Definition 1.9 An S-box $S : \{0, 1\}^n \to \{0, 1\}^m$ has correlation immunity (respectively resiliency) of order k if all Boolean functions $\{\mathbf{c} \cdot S(\mathbf{x}) : \mathbf{c} \neq \mathbf{0}\}$ have correlation immunity (resiliency) of order k.

To study all these properties of S-box, we need to find the Walsh–Hadamard transform values of each linear combination $\mathbf{c} \cdot S(\mathbf{x})$, where $c \neq \mathbf{0}$. The Walsh–Hadamard transform of $\mathbf{c} \cdot S(\mathbf{x})$, where $\mathbf{c} \neq \mathbf{0}$ will be,

$$\mathcal{W}_S(\mathbf{c}, \mathbf{a}) = \sum_{\mathbf{x} \in \{0,1\}^n} (-1)^{\mathbf{c} \cdot S(\mathbf{x}) \oplus \mathbf{a} \cdot \mathbf{x}}, \text{ where } \mathbf{c} \in \{0, 1\}^m, \ \mathbf{a} \in \{0, 1\}^n. \qquad (1.3)$$

For an S-box $S : \{0, 1\}^n \to \{0, 1\}^m$, the relation between nonlinearity and Walsh–Hadamard transformation will be,

$$nl(S) = 2^{n-1} - \frac{1}{2} \max_{\mathbf{c},\mathbf{a}} \left| \mathcal{W}_S(\mathbf{c}, \mathbf{a}) \right|, \text{ where } \mathbf{c} \in \{0, 1\}^m, \ \mathbf{a} \in \{0, 1\}^n.$$

Similarly, if the S-box S has correlation immunity k then,

$$\mathcal{W}_S(\mathbf{c}, \mathbf{a}) = 0, \text{ for all } 1 \leq wt(\mathbf{a}) \leq k, \ \mathbf{a} \in \{0, 1\}^n \text{ and } \mathbf{c} \neq \mathbf{0}, \mathbf{c} \in \{0, 1\}^m.$$

The weight 0 inputs should also be considered for resiliency, i.e., it includes balancedness over and above correlation immunity.

Now let us define derivative of an S-box. However, before that, let us consider the autocorrelation (Preneel et al. 1991; Zhang and Zheng 1995) property of a Boolean function. Let $\beta \in \{0, 1\}^n$. The autocorrelation value of the Boolean function f with respect to the vector $\beta \in \{0, 1\}^n$ is

$$\Delta_f(\beta) = \sum_{x \in \{0,1\}^n} (-1)^{f(x) \oplus f(x \oplus \beta)}.$$

Further, we denote

$$\Delta_f = \max_{\beta \in \{0,1\}^n, \beta \neq (0,\dots,0)} |\Delta_f(\beta)|$$

and Δ_f is called the absolute indicator. The function f is said to satisfy $PC(k)$, if $\Delta_f(\beta) = 0$ for $1 \leq wt(\beta) \leq k$.

A function f is said to satisfy SAC if $f(x) \oplus f(x \oplus \alpha)$ is balanced for any α such that $wt(\alpha) = 1$. Further, f is said to satisfy $SAC(k)$ if any function obtained from f by keeping any k input bits constant satisfies SAC. With this background, let us now concentrate on S-boxes, i.e., multiple output Boolean functions.

Definition 1.10 Let $S : \{0, 1\}^n \to \{0, 1\}^m$ be an S-box. The derivative of S with respect to $\mathbf{a} \in \{0, 1\}^n$ is

$$\Delta_{\mathbf{a}}^S(\mathbf{x}) = S(\mathbf{x} \oplus \mathbf{a}) \oplus S(\mathbf{x}).$$

It can be observed that $\Delta_{\mathbf{a}}^S$ is a two-dimensional array which is known as difference distribution table. Below we define differential uniformity of S-box from the derivative of S-box.

Definition 1.11 Let $S : \{0, 1\}^n \to \{0, 1\}^m$ be an S-box and $\delta_S(\mathbf{a}, \mathbf{b}) = \left| \{\mathbf{x} \in \{0, 1\}^n\} : \Delta_{\mathbf{a}}^S(\mathbf{x}) = \mathbf{b} \right|$. The differential uniformity of S is $\max_{\mathbf{a},\mathbf{b}} \delta_S(\mathbf{a}, \mathbf{b})$, where $\mathbf{a} \in \{0, 1\}^n$, $\mathbf{b} \in \{0, 1\}^m$.

Here, we consider an example of S-box to study these properties.

Example 1.7 Let $S : \{0, 1\}^4 \rightarrow \{0, 1\}^4$, where $S = [10, 6, 5, 1, 9, 0, 12, 14, 4, 13, 15, 7, 3, 8, 11, 2]$. The coordinate functions are $f_1 = x_0 x_1 x_2 \oplus x_0 x_1 x_3 \oplus x_0 x_2 x_3 \oplus x_0 x_2 \oplus x_0 x_3 \oplus x_1 x_2 x_3 \oplus x_1 \oplus x_2$, $f_2 = x_0 x_1 x_2 \oplus x_0 x_2 x_3 \oplus x_1 x_2 \oplus x_1 \oplus x_2 \oplus x_3 \oplus 1$, $f_3 = x_0 x_1 x_3 \oplus x_0 x_2 \oplus x_0 x_3 \oplus x_1 x_2 x_3 \oplus x_1 x_2 \oplus x_3 \oplus 1$, and $f_4 = x_0 x_2 x_3 \oplus x_0 x_2 \oplus x_0 x_3 \oplus x_0 \oplus x_1 x_3 \oplus x_1 \oplus x_2 x_3 \oplus x_3$. The degree of this S-box is 3, nonlinearity is 2 and differential uniformity is 6.

Finally, let us briefly discuss about algebraic immunity (Courtois and Meier 2003). We have already discussed the importance of high algebraic degree. Moreover, to resist algebraic attack, the function should not have a low degree multiple (Courtois and Meier 2003; Meier et al. 2004). It is shown (Courtois and Meier 2003) that given any n-variable Boolean function f, it is always possible to get a Boolean function g with degree at most $\lceil \frac{n}{2} \rceil$ such that fg is of degree at most $\lceil \frac{n}{2} \rceil$. Here, the functions are considered to be multivariate polynomials over $GF(2)$ and fg is the polynomial multiplication over $GF(2)$. In other words, this is the AND operation between f and g, i.e., the truth table of fg is bitwise AND of the truth tables of f, g.

1. Given $f \in B_n$, a nonzero function $g \in B_n$ is called an annihilator of f if $fg = 0$. By $AN(f)$ we mean the set of annihilators of f.
2. Given $f \in B_n$, the algebraic immunity of f, denoted by $\mathcal{AI}_n(f) = \deg(g)$, where $g \in B_n$ is the minimum degree nonzero function such that either $fg = 0$ or $(1 + f)g = 0$.

It is known (Courtois and Meier 2003; Meier et al. 2004) that for $f \in B_n$, $\mathcal{AI}_n(f) \leq \lceil \frac{n}{2} \rceil$. As in the previous cases, this definition can be suitably extended for S-boxes with all possible non-zero linear combinations of the co-ordinate functions.

Having covered these prerequisites, we can now analyze cryptographic properties of the stream ciphers based on the aforementioned models. One such cipher is ZUC stream cipher, which is used in Long-Term Evolution (LTE) standards, which is a part of mobile telephony. The LTE standard was developed by Third-Generation Partnership Project (3GPP) (2020).

1.6 Overview on 3GPP and Where ZUC Stands

The Third-Generation Partnership Project (3GPP) (2020) was initiated by the European Telecommunications Standards Institute (ETSI) in 1998 with the goal of developing new technologies for third generation (3G) of cellular network. The 3GPP is responsible for the development of faster telephony standards over the last two decades. We give a brief description of the structure of the organization to get readers familiar with the world of mobile telephony. The organizational partners of 3GPP are Association of Radio Industries and Businesses (ARIB) and Telecommunication Technology Committee (TTC) from Japan, Alliance for Telecommunications Industry Solutions (ATIS) from USA, China Communications Standards Association (CCSA) from China, European Telecommunications Standards Institute (ETSI) from Europe, Telecommunications Standards Development Society (TSDSI) from India and Telecommunications Technology Association (TTA) from South Korea. These partners approve and maintain several tasks such as scope of the project, description of the project and several other technical details.

The development of 3GPP is driven by a member of companies in Working Groups (WGs) and in the Technical Specification Groups (TSGs). The TSGs of 3GPP are Radio Access Networks (RAN), Services and Systems Aspects (SA), Core Network and Terminals (CT).

The prime focus of all 3GPP releases is to make the system backward and forward compatible where it is possible. This feature ensures that the operation of user equipment avoids interruption. Several international companies and their groups have participated in this project. The initial development of 3G technology was heavily influenced by 2G GSM standard. At the end, 3GPP tends to use CDMA technology as a base for 3G technology, although CDMA technology and 3G technology have differences. One can go through (3rd Generation Partnership Project 2020) for more details. The 3G technology was called W-CDMA or UTM. Concurrently, another team from the United States parallely developed 3GPP2. The baseline of this technology was also CDMA. 3GPP2 technology was called CDMA2000. Both these technologies 3GPP and 3GPP2 were approved by International Telecommunication Union (ITU) for 3G technology. Further, this 3G technology has been developed gradually to provide data-optimized technologies which are known as 3GPP2 EV-DO, 3GPP HSPA. These are being used all over the world.

In the mid-2000, the development process of 4G standards was started. The 3GPP developed a standard called LTE for this. Several other organizations such as 3GPP2 and IEEE also formed their own standards. Among these developed standards, the LTE developed by 3GPP became the official standard for 4G. This standard is now being used in all 4G carriers over the world. Since early 2010, 3GPP has been developing a standard called New Radio for the fifth generation of mobile architecture.

1.6.1 ZUC

The 3GPP Systems and Architecture Group (SA3) agreed in May 2009 to accept a new encryption and integrity algorithm set designed in China. The possible motivation is that the Chinese authorities would permit its use in that country. The algorithm set is based on the stream cipher ZUC, named after Zu Chongzhi, a famous Chinese scientist (429–500 AD). While the politics and history behind the cipher might be very interesting, that is not in the scope of this book. However, it is very clear that "an algorithm from China" cannot be a technical requirement. Thus, the cipher was designed and evaluated with proper methodology. The initial design was proposed by experts from the Data Assurance and Communication Security Research Centre (DACAS) at the Chinese Academy of Science.

Two confidentiality and integrity algorithm sets had been developed and standardized for LTE before the third one. The first one, 128-EEA1 and 128-EIA1, is based on the stream cipher SNOW 3G, and was inherited from the UMTS network. The second set, 128-EEA2 and 128-EIA2, is based on the internationally accepted block cipher AES (Advanced Encryption Standard). As per the decision of 3GPP SA3, the third set, 128-EEA3 and 128-EIA3, has been designed. The 128-EEA3 is the LTE encryption algorithm defined using ZUC and the 128-EIA3 is the LTE integrity algorithm, designed as a Universal Hash Function using ZUC as its core.

Let us quickly present the view of SAGE (Security Algorithms Group of Experts) on ZUC.

- One stated objective for the design was that the new algorithms be substantially different from the first and second LTE algorithm sets, in such a way that an attack on any one algorithm set would be unlikely to lead to an attack on either of the others.
- In SAGE's view this objective is not fully met—there are some architectural similarities between ZUC and SNOW 3G, and it is possible that a major advance in cryptanalysis might affect them both.
- However, there are important differences too, so ZUC and SNOW 3G by no means "stand or fall together".

In Chaps. 4 and 5, we try to understand what are the technical reasons that may motivate a cryptographer to design a stream cipher like ZUC.

1.7 Confidentiality and Integrity Using Stream Cipher

We are already familiar of the terminologies confidentiality and integrity (for definition see Sect. 1.1). The confidentiality algorithm is used to hide the content of the message from an unauthorized person, whereas the integrity algorithm provides the receiver with tools to identify the correctness of the received message. One can design such algorithm using a stream cipher.

A stream cipher is basically based on a pseudo-random bit (number) generator G, which generates random looking output using an initial seed as input. These output bits are further XORed with the message bits to generate the corresponding ciphertext bits. If the receiving person is having the same initial seed then (s)he will be able to generate same bit (number) by using the same pseudo-random bit (number) generator G, which (s)he can XOR with ciphertext to recover the plaintext. The initial seed is considered as the secret key K shared between sender and receiver. If this key is unknown to any other person then (s)he will not be able to recover the plaintext from ciphertext. This process enables the confidentiality.

As a pseudo-random generator has the property that, if we give the same input, it will generate the same output. Hence, same secret key is used in G to generate keystream to encrypt different messages then it will not be secure. As the encryption mechanism of a stream cipher is based on one time padding encryption technique. To overcome this issue, another parameter is introduced, which is known as initialization vector IV. Instead of taking only one parameter K as input, the pseudo-random generator G will take K, IV as input. Further, it performs a mixing process which is known as key scheduling process, where pseudo-random generator G mixes the secret key K and initialization vector IV. After that, it generates keystream which will be used to encrypt the message. After encrypting the message the sender will send the ciphertext and the used initialization vector IV to receiver over public channel. Receiver uses the received IV and performs the same procedure and generates same keystream to decrypt the received ciphertext. As the initialization vector IV is transmitted over public channel, hence can be changed for different messages. This provides flexibility in encrypting different messages using same key.

The integrity security attribute allows the receiver to check the correctness of the received message. For doing that, the one will require a message authentication code (MAC) generation mechanism. In literature, there are several constrictions of MAC generation algorithms. The first novel construction of MAC using stream cipher was proposed by Krawczyk (1994). The construction of MAC described in Krawczyk (1994) is based on LSFR. Here, we give the idea of the construction. Before that, we describe a hashing mechanism based on Boolean matrix. Suppose H is an $n \times m$ Boolean matrix and M is a message containing m bits. The hash value of M with respect to the matrix H will be the Boolean matrix multiplication of the matrix H by the column vector consists of bits of message M.

$$h_H(M) = H \cdot M, \text{ where } H \text{ is a } n \times m \text{ matrix, and } M \text{ is an } m \times 1 \text{ matrix.}$$

The family of functions $\{h_H : H \text{ is a } n \times m \text{ Boolean matrix }\}$ is known a universal family of hash functions.

Now we describe, the construction of MAC algorithm based on LFSR proposed in Krawczyk (1994). Suppose $p(x)$ be an irreducible polynomial over $GF(2)$ of degree n. Consider an LFSR with the feedback polynomial $p(x)$. Let $s_0, s_1, \ldots$ be the output bit generated by the LFSR, where the initial state is $S = (s_0, s_1, \ldots, s_{n-1})$. For each polynomial $p(x)$ and a non-zero initial state S, one can associate a universal hashing mechanism $h_{p,s}$ on message $M = (m_0, \ldots, m_{m-1})$, which is defined below.

$$h_{p,s}(M) = \oplus_{j=0}^{m-1} m_j \cdot (s_j, s_{j+1}, \cdots, s_{j+n-1}).$$

Fig. 1.4 Construction of MAC using LFSR

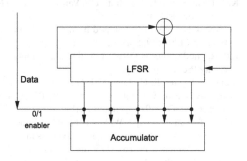

The $h_{p,s}(M)$ is considered as message authentication code of the message M. From this MAC, one can check the integrity of the received message. In Fig. 1.4, we provide an example of such a construction.

We consider a communication system where confidentiality and integrity algorithm both are implemented. In this scenario, the sender will send ciphertext and MAC of the original message to receiver over public channel. Receiver after receiving ciphertext and MAC, he/she will first perform decryption on ciphertext. Further, he/she generates the MAC by performing same integrity algorithm on the decrypted message. If the received MAC and computed MAC matches with each other, then the receiver will convince that the received message was not altered during communication.

References

3rd Generation Partnership Project (3GPP): https://www.3gpp.org/

Specification of the 3GPP Confidentiality and Integrity Algorithms 128-EEA3 and 128-EIA3. ETSI/SAGE, Document 2: ZUC Specification, Version 1.6, 28th June, 2011. https://www.gsma.com/aboutus/wp-content/uploads/2014/12/eea3eia3zucv16.pdf

National Bureau of Standards. Data Encryption Standard, FIPS-Pub.46. National Bureau of Standards, U.S. Department of Commerce, Washington D.C., January 1977

Blum L, Blum M, Shub M (1986) A simple unpredictable random number generator. SIAM J Comput 15:364–383

Courtois N, Meier W (2003) Algebraic attacks on stream ciphers with linear feedback. In: Advances in Cryptology - EUROCRYPT 2003, Number 2656 in Lecture notes in computer science, pp 345–359. Springer, Berlin

Cusick TW, Stănică P (2017) Cryptographic Boolean functions and applications. Academic, New York

Daemen J, Rijmen V (2001) AES proposal: Rijndael. National Institute of Standards and Technology

Ding C, Xiao G, Shan W (1991) The stability theory of stream ciphers. Number 561 in Lecture notes in computer science. Springer, Berlin

Golomb SW (1967) Shift register sequences. Holden-Day, San Fransisco

Guo-Zhen X, Massey J (1988) A spectral characterization of correlation immune combining functions. IEEE Trans Inf Theory 34(3):569–571

Hell M, Johansson T, Meier W (2020) Grain - a stream cipher for constrained environments. https://www.ecrypt.eu.org/stream/p3ciphers/grain/Grain_p3.pdf

Katz J, Menezes AJ, Oorschot PCV, Vanstone SA (1996) Handbook of applied cryptography. CRC Press, Boca Raton

Krawczyk H (1994) LFSR-based hashing and authentication. Advances in cryptology (CRYPTO 1994), pp 129–139, Springer, Berlin

Lidl R, Niederreiter H (1994) Introduction to finite fields and their applications. Cambridge University Press, Cambridge

Meier W, Pasalic E, Carlet C (2004) Algebraic attacks and decomposition of Boolean functions. In: Advances in Cryptology - EUROCRYPT 2004, Number 3027 in Lecture notes in computer science, pp 474–491. Springer, Berlin

Preneel B, Van Leekwijck W, Van Linden L, Govaerts R, Vandewalle J (1991) Propagation characteristics of Boolean functions. In: Advances in Cryptology - EUROCRYPT'90, Lecture notes in computer science, pp 161–173. Springer, Berlin

Rueppel RA (1986) Analysis and design of stream ciphers. Springer, Berlin

Rueppel RA, Staffelbach OJ (1987) Products of linear recurring sequences with maximum complexity. IEEE Trans Inf Theory IT-33:124–131

Sarkar P (2002) The filter-combiner model for memoryless synchronous stream ciphers. In: Annual international cryptology conference (CRYPTO 2002), pp 533–584. Springer

Siegenthaler T (1984) Correlation-immunity of nonlinear combining functions for cryptographic applications. IEEE Trans Inf Theory IT-30(5):776–780

Siegenthaler T (1985) Decrypting a class of stream ciphers using ciphertext only. IEEE Trans Comput C-34(1):81–85

Zhang XM, Zheng Y (1995) GAC - the criterion for global avalanche characteristics of cryptographic functions. J Univ Comput Sci 1(5):316–333

Chapter 2
Telephony Architecture

Abstract In this chapter, we discuss how data transmission is handled in different generations of telephony and how the encryption and decryption of the data take place. We look at the architecture of different standards and the encryption as well as authentication protocols.

Keywords Telephony · GSM · 3G · 4G · LTE · 5G

2.1 Outline of Security Protocols

The security protocol in telephony architecture is divided into two or three primary steps depending on the generation. The first step is authentication, where the end user is authenticated by the network. In the higher generations of telephony, the end user also authenticates the network. In GSM architecture, after authentication is done, data is encrypted using the confidentiality algorithm and transmitted. In higher generations, an integrity algorithm is also used to ensure the integrity of the data. The integrity algorithm checks if the data received by the end user or the stations connected to the network has been modified in any way. This secures the communication from intervention by a false station.

In the next section, we describe the architecture of the different generations of telephony to have a basic understanding of the procedure of transmission of data. We also describe the channel where the data encryption takes place, and describe the authentication process. We selectively discuss the details of integrity and confidentiality algorithm for one of the standards in later chapters.

2.2 The Architecture of the Different Generations

The architecture of mobile telephony varies with different generations. We first start with the architecture of GSM.

© The Author(s), under exclusive license to Springer Nature Singapore Pte Ltd. 2021   27
C. S. Mukherjee et al., *Design and Cryptanalysis of ZUC*,
SpringerBriefs on Cyber Security Systems and Networks,
https://doi.org/10.1007/978-981-33-4882-0_2

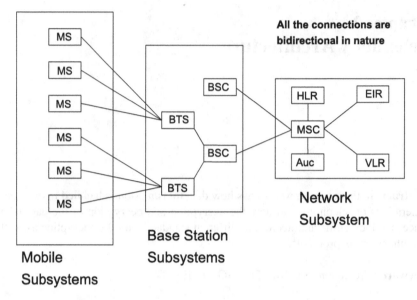

Fig. 2.1 GSM architecture

2.2.1   GSM/2G

GSM (2G) is the first generation of telephony that supports digital encryption. The encryption is done while communicating the data from a mobile equipment to a base station receiver. Encryption in 2G telephony marked the beginning of a new era, where the conversations couldn't be tapped by anyone, even after reading the signals sent from a mobile equipment. However, the situation is not so simple. For example, the A5/1 stream cipher is in use in such a system and it is well known that the communications through this setup can be immediately broken (Decryption 2020). In fact, that is the reason, worldwide efforts are continuously going on toward more secure encryption.

Let us now explain the network structure of the GSM architecture (Digital cellular telecommunications system 2020). This structure is responsible for the actual transmission of the data in encrypted form and successful completion of said transmission. It is divided into three components as shown in the Fig. 2.1.

1. **The mobile station:** It refers to the individual end user systems at operation. The mobile system consists of the mobile equipment, which is the physical device in use and the Subscriber Identity Module, which is commonly known by its acronym, SIM. The SIM plays a very important role in terms of encryption and decryption of the transmitted data, and also in the authentication of the made calls by the network subsystem. The SIM contains the secret key which is essential to the encryption of data and also generates the session keys, that are put into the encryption algorithms.

Table 2.1 A few components of GSM

Component	Description
Home Location Register (HLR)	The HLR stores all the data of all subscribers being served by its corresponding MSC
Visitor Location Register (VLR)	The VLR contains the data of all the mobiles connected to its corresponding MSC at a any point of time
Equipment Identity Register (EIR)	The EIR stores the international mobile equipment identities of all the mobile stations and maintains whether a particular mobile station is trustworthy or not

2. **The base station subsystem:** It integrates the mobile stations to the network and acts as entry points for any calls. This layer consists of two parts, the base transceiver stations and the base station controllers.

   a. **The Base Transceiver Station (BTS):** The BTS are the physical stations that the mobile stations transmit their data to. The connectivity of a mobile station is dependent on the distance of the nearest BTS and whether the mobile station is able to establish communication with the BTS.

   b. **Base station controllers:** The BSCs control a certain number of BTS as a part of the hierarchical layer wise architecture that forms the backbone of the GSM network.

3. **The Network Subsystem (NS):** The main purpose of the network subsystem is to route calls between different BSCs in different regions and to authenticate calls and maintain the database of subscribers, the history of the transmission of data and bills corresponding to each subscriber. It has different components which are responsible for carrying out these tasks. They are as follows:

   a. **Mobile Switching center (MSC):** The MSC is responsible for routing of calls and thus is in control of a large number of BSCs. This takes care of the routing needed for the transmission of data between two mobile stations.

   b. **Authentication Center (Auc):** The Authentication center ensures integrity and trustability of the transmitted data. It contains the permanent secret key corresponding to each SIM and also generates the Random challenges that are needed for authentication of a connection.

Table 2.1 gives a brief description of all the components of the network subsystem.

2.2.1.1 Security in GSM Network

Security in GSM is divided into two parts, namely authentication and confidentiality. The data is encrypted only between the mobile station and the base station. It means

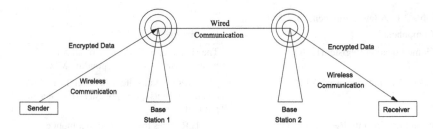

Fig. 2.2 Mobile security architecture

that when data is sent to a base station from a mobile station, it is encrypted in the mobile station and then decrypted at the base station. The data then reaches the base station closest to the end receiver in the plaintext form. It is again encrypted there and then sent to the mobile station, where it is decrypted. The Fig. 2.2 gives a brief overview of this protocol. This methodology is also maintained in the higher generations.

Both authentication of a connection and the subsequent formation of the session key are handled by the COMP128 algorithm (Briceno 2020). This algorithm is also referred to as A3/A8 algorithm depending on where it is used.

2.2.1.2 Authentication

During the establishment of a call, the end users need to be authenticated by the NS and Auc of NS handles this operation. Every SIM has a secret key, which is the identity key of the SIM. This detail is also stored in the Auc. When a connection is being established, the NS sends a random 128-bit number to the corresponding SIM. The SIM then mixes the random number with the secret key using the A3 algorithm to form a response named SRES and sends it to the Auc via the network. The Auc meanwhile also runs the COMP128 algorithm using the secret key designated to the SIM and the random number and generates a value on its own. Then the SRES sent by the mobile equipment and the value generated by the Auc are matched, and a successful match implies a successful establishment of the connection.

2.2.1.3 Confidentiality

The session key is created and used for the duration of one call, and a 64-bit session key is created using the COMP128 algorithm. The COMP128 algorithm takes the 128-bit permanent key stored in the SIM and the 128-bit random number sent by the NS and generates a 64-bit session key. This key is then fed into the confidentiality algorithms for encryption of the call. The session key is fed into the confidentiality algorithm which is situated in the hardware terminal and not in the SIM.

The session key along with the publicly known frame number (also known as the initialization vector) is fed into the confidentiality algorithm. In GSM, a frame is sent every 4.6 milliseconds. A frame consists of 228 bits of data, 114 bits in the up-link and 114 bits in the down-link. It means that the algorithm must produce 228 bits of data per frame, and half of it used for encryption of data which will be sent, and the other half for decryption for incoming data. This is the reason behind the algorithm being situated in the hardware terminal, to ensure fast implementation. This method of the algorithms being situated in the hardware terminal has been carried out in all the future generations of mobile telephony as well. GSM has three confidentiality algorithms, they are as follows:

1. **A5/0:** It actually does not provide any encryption and it is just a placeholder as per standards requirement.
2. **A5/1:** It was defined as a secure algorithm of GSM (which is presently not true). It is a stream cipher that takes in a 64-bit key and the frame number, known as the initialization vector.
3. **A5/2:** It is a slightly weaker version of A5/1 and is used in countries where the government wants to selectively monitor calls with fair ease.

2.2.2 UMTS/3G

The third generation saw a shift from a focus on mobile voice connectivity to data transmission rates, and connectivity in general. That also propelled a change in terminology, to mark the broader use of the network, as opposed to the 2G voice telephony, which was restricted to mobile telephone devices. The UMTS (Universal Mobile Telecommunications System) network can also be used by a laptop or a desktop for using its internet connectivity. The architecture is the same as GSM, with certain enhancements in data transmission and security (Universal Mobile Telecommunications System 2020a). The main addition in data transmission is that in UMTS, voice and data are routed in the core network via different components. Voice calls are transmitted in the same way as in GSM, using circuit-based switching using equivalents of Mobile Switching Centers (MSC).

The other method of switching used is packet-based switching, which is handled by SGSN and GGSN. SGSN stands for Serving GPRS Support Node and is introduced as part of the GPRS standard which first enabled the internet connectivity, and is treated as an intermediate stage between GSM and UMTS. The SGSN is connected to the base stations in the intermediate layer and is then the data is relayed to the Gateway GPRS Support Node (GGSN), which routes the data to the end-user via SGSN and radio network controllers that connects to the receiving end. The radio network controllers and SGSN are together called to be the serving network. The UMTS architecture (Fig. 2.3) can be broken down into the following layers.

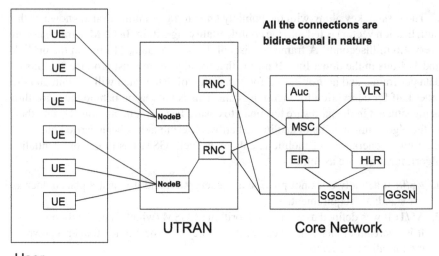

Fig. 2.3 UMTS architecture

1. **User Equipment:** This is the equivalent of the mobile equipment of the GSM network and consists of the Universal Subscriber Identity Module (USIM) and the end-user device.
2. **UMTS Radio Network Subsystem:** Is is also known as the Universal Terrestrial Radio Access Network (UTRAN). This is equivalent to the base station subsystem of the GSM architecture. UTRAN consists of two components, enodeB, which is the equivalent of BTS in GSM and Radio Network controller (RNC) which connects the enodeB with the core network, like BSC in GSM. It is important to note that UMTS also supports the GSM architecture and the voice calls are often transmitted using the GSM architecture. This is called backward compatibility and is available in the future generations as well. In fact, in the higher generation, a lot of the times the voice calls are carried over the architectures of older generations, and only the internet data is transmitted over the most recent and fast architecture.
3. **The core network:** The core network is the central network which handles authentication, maintaining data sets related to the users and routing of data throughout the network. It contains all the components that the Network Subsystem does in GSM network.

2.2.2.1 Security in 3G

The notion of security is same in UMTS as in GSM in the sense that the data is only encrypted between the user equipment and the connecting Radio Network Controller (RNC), the RNC being equivalent to base stations in GSM. The improvement in the architecture is that the authentication is both ways in UMTS (Universal Mobile Telecommunications System 2020b). In UMTS, the RNC authenticates the user equipment, and the user equipment authenticates the RNC, ensuring a greater degree of security. The confidentiality algorithms used are also different from GSM. Here, the confidentiality algorithm is based on KASUMI (also known as A5/3) and SNOW 3G. The main difference is that, while A5/1 only had 64-bit session keys, KASUMI and SNOW 3G in UMTS use 128-bit key and thus provide much better security.

UMTS provides two-way authentication. The authentication and the key generation procedures start simultaneously. The authentication takes place between Auc of the core network and the USIM. Both entities share some components that are used to complete the authentication process. They are as follows:

1. A permanent key (say pK), that is the identity of the USIM. This key is also shared with the Auc.
2. Authentication function f_1 and f_2.
3. Key generating functions f_3, f_4, f_5.

The main enhancement in UMTS in terms of authentication is the addition of the Anonymity key (AK), the generated sequence (SQN) and the integrity key (IK). We now describe the authentication process and describe the new variables as they are introduced into the procedure. The authentication process is started by an authentication request by the serving network, following which the Auc generates a random number $(RAND)$ and a previously unused sequence (SQN). The SQN plays a very important role in this authentication process. The procedure to create SQN is time-variant and operator-specific. Thus, the SQN certifies the freshness of the other generated values. The Auc then uses the permanent key K associated with the corresponding USIM and an Authentication Management Field (AMF) to create the following values.

1. $MAC = f_1(SQN \parallel RAND \parallel AMF, K)$,
2. $XRES = f_2(RAND, K)$,
3. $CK = f_3(RAND, K)$,
4. $IK = f_4(RAND, K)$,
5. $AK = f_5(RAND, K)$.

Then an authentication token $AUTN$ is created, where $AUTN = (SQN \oplus AK) \parallel AMF \parallel MAC$. The reasoning behind this is that AK masks the SQN variable, which can leak information about the identity of the user. After $AUTN$ is created, it is sent together with $XRES$, CK and IK to the user by forming the variable AV, where $AV = RAND \parallel XRES \parallel CK \parallel IK \parallel AUTN$. Once AV reaches the user, the authentication is done in the following steps. If any of the comparisons fail, the authentication is terminated without going to the next step.

1. AK is derived using $AK = f_5(RAND, K)$.
2. Then SQN is found as $SQN \oplus AK$ is sent in the authentication token.

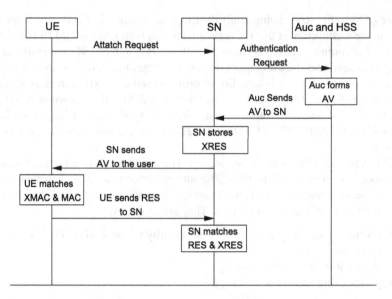

Fig. 2.4 Authentication in UMTS

3. As AMF is also sent to the user, two variables $XMAC$ and RES are computed using the values of SQN and AK.
4. $XMAC = f_1(SQN \parallel RAND \parallel AMF, K)$
5. Then the value of $XMAC$ is matched with MAC, which has been sent from Auc as part of $AUTN$.
6. If the values are matched, then the integrity of SQN is confirmed by checking if its in the correct range.
7. CK and IK are calculated using f_4 and f_5 respectively.
8. RES is then calculated as $RES = f_2(RAND, K)$. Then it is sent to the serving node (SGSN) as part of the authentication procedure which is similar to that of GSM architecture. If the SGSN matches RES with $XRES$ that it received from the Auc, then a successful match completes the successful authentication process.

The flowchart in Fig. 2.4 gives an overview of the authentication protocol. This approach essentially removes the threat of fake base station vulnerability in GSM which took advantage of the fact that the user equipment does not authenticate the base station in GSM. This is because MAC is a function of SQN, Key and $RAND$. Although the random variable ($RAND$) can be intercepted. As SQN keeps changing with time, deducing key from just the information of $RAND$ becomes very difficult. The integrity key (IK) is used in the integration protection module and the session key (CK) is used in the confidentiality algorithm for encryption of the data to be transmitted. We discuss these two procedures in detail in the later section.

2.2.3 LTE/4G Architecture

The first radical change that marked the formation of the fourth-generation architecture was removing all circuit-based switching entities. In the LTE architecture, both voice calls and data transmission are handled via a packet-based switching entity, which implies that 4G is completely internet protocol (IP)-based.

In the LTE standard, the network is broken into components a little differently. The end user devices and the controllers and transceiver stations are together called the Evolved Universal Terrestrial Radio Access Network (E-UTRAN) which is then connected to the core network, which is further connected with the IP network (LTE 2020). The serving network and the home network constitute to be the core network. The main entities of the 4G LTE architecture are as follows.

1. **User Equipment (UE):** The User Equipment are the end user devices in use along with the integrity modules. It contains the UICC (Universal Integrated Circuit Card) and USIM (Universal Subscriber Integrity Module). The UE contains the permanent secret key that is essential to authentication, integrity evaluation and encryption.
2. **Evolved NodeB (enodeB):** The evolved nodeB connects the UEs to the core network. In 4G-LTE structure, the enodeBs are directly connected to the core network, which increases the speed of communication.
3. **Mobile Management Entity (MME):** The Mobile Management Entity controls all the enodeBs and connects the UE and the home network. The MME also handles routing of the data and keeps track of the UE location.
4. **Home Subscriber Server (HSS):** The Home Subscriber Server serves the purpose of both the Auc and HLR in the previous generations, by handling the database related to the users and their permanent secret keys. It also participates in the authentication process and creates the authentication vectors (AV) that are then sent to the MME.
5. **Packet Data Network Gateway (P-Gw):** The P-Gw connects the core network to the IP network.
6. **Serving Gateway(S-Gw):** The Serving Gateways are responsible for routing the data to the UE. An S-Gw serves a particular zone and reduces the usage of the P-Gw.

Figure 2.5 describes the LTE architecture.

2.2.3.1 Security in 4G

The authentication in 4G is handled by the Authentication and Key Agreement (AKA) protocol (A Comparative Introduction to 4G and 5G Authentication 2020). Authentication in 4G is started by an attached message request by the user equipment to the MME. The attached message is either the IMSI value or a temporary value, called GUTI assigned to the UE to reduce the frequency of transmission of the sensitive

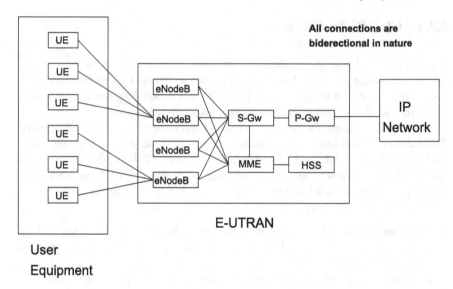

Fig. 2.5 GSM architecture

IMSI detail over the radio network. If GUTI is sent by the UE, then the GUTI is authenticated and the process continues. If, for some reason, the GUTI is not authenticated, then the MME asks for the IMSI. After it is verified, the process moves in to the next step. After this, the MME forward the authentication request to the HSS. The process after this step is same as that in UMTS authentication process. The MME is the equivalent of the serving network and the HSS is the equivalent of the Auc.

The change introduced in 4G is the addition of they key K_{ASME}, which is generated by using the CK, IK, SQN and a new entity called the $SnId$, which is a serving network-specific id corresponding to the UE. This key serves as a local master key for the connection. Then HSS executes the following steps:

1. The HSS generates a random challenge, called $RAND$.
2. The CK and IK are generated using the permanent key K.
3. A sequence number corresponding to the UE is generated by SQN, which ensures freshness of the authentication vector (AV) to be sent.
4. The MAC and $XRES$ are generated as in UMTS.
5. The K_{ASME} is created using a key derivation function which takes the CK, IK and the $SQN \oplus AK$ value. This is an improvement on the UMTS authentication protocol as the CK and IK values are not sent without protection.
6. Then the authentication vector is created in the MME which contains the $MAC, XRES, K_{ASME}, RAND, SQN$ values and is sent to the UE via the MME.
7. The MME keeps the K_{ASME} and the $XRES$ values for the authentication and sends the AV to UE.
8. The UE generates all the values as in UMTS to form $XMAC$ and RES and checks whether SQN is in the correct range or not.

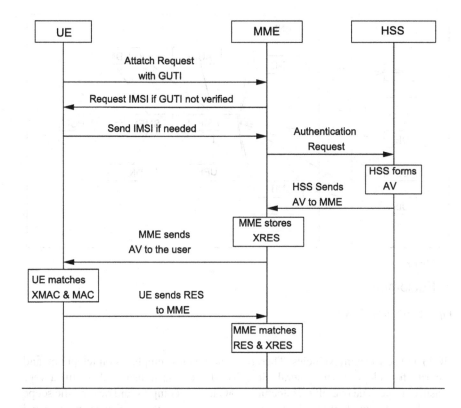

Fig. 2.6 Authentication in LTE

9. Then the UE sends the RES value to the MME which matches it with the $XRES$ value and a successful match implies completion of the authentication process.

One can refer to the flowchart in Fig. 2.6 for getting an overview of the process. Once the authentication process is completed, the integrity module and the confidentiality algorithms start their respective procedures.

2.2.4 New Radio (NR)/5G

The 5G technology is the most recent and advanced generation of telecommunication network and is under implementation and development in several countries. The fifth generation offers a huge speedup in data transmission rates. It is expected to deliver speeds of up to 100 GBPS, which is about a hundred times faster than the speed offered by 4G. The 5G is expected to be used in a multitude of scenarios, ranging from normal surfing of the internet to transmission of data in the Internet of Things

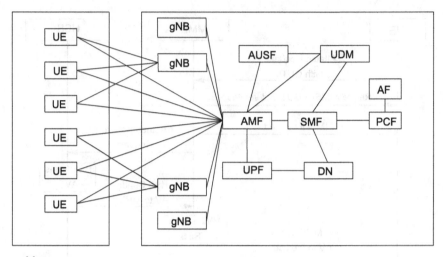

User

Equipment

Fig. 2.7 5G architecture

(IOT) and self-driving vehicles. Therefore, there is less emphasis on telephony and security for telephony in general. Security of the data transmitted is still a very sensitive issue. The overall architecture of 5G is very complex and beyond the scope of the book. So we shall only look at the architecture from a security perspective and note the improvements and differences from the LTE architecture.

2.2.4.1   5G Architecture

Some components of the 4G architecture has been replaced with new systems in 5G (ETSI TS 2020). For example, the base station in 5G is denoted as gNB, which stands for Next-Generation Node B, and it houses the new radio system of 5G. The Mobile Management Entity (MME) has been broken down into Access and Mobility Management Function (AMF) which takes care of all the connection related works and the Session Management Function (SMF) which handles all the messages related to any active session. Figure 2.7 gives a brief overview of the 5G architecture.

The 5G architecture has also seen some improvement in the authentication procedure (A Comparative Introduction to 4G and 5G Authentication 2020). There are two weaknesses of 4G that have been addressed in the newest architecture. As we have discussed, a value called GUTI is used in 4G to reduce the frequency of transmission of the sensitive SUPI value. SUPI stands for Subscriber Permanent Identifier and is the equivalent of the IMSI value in the earlier generations. However, it has been shown that this procedure is not very effective and doesn't reliably hide the IMSI

(SUPI) information, as the 4G architecture has the option to send the SUPI value if the GUTI value is not accepted. The second weakness is that the home network does not participate in the authentication. It does provide the serving network with the authentication vector, but the decision is solely taken by the serving network. These weaknesses are mitigated in 5G in the following ways.

2.2.4.2 Authentication in 5G

The first change is that the decision capacity for authentication is shifted to the home network. The second change is that there are more than one authentication procedures defined under the 5G architecture to serve under different scenarios. We describe these newly introduced entities and their use in the authentication protocol. Some new entities are added to incorporate these new functionalities. These entities are as follows.

1. **Unified Data Management (UDM):** This entity manages the data related to all the authentication protocols and also generates the integrity key, confidentiality key and the authentication vector, which are required to complete the authentication protocol.
2. **The Security Anchor Function (SEAF):** This function is added in the serving network. The serving network still retains the ability to reject authentication request coming from the User Equipment, but the home network has the final decision on whether to accept an authentication request or not.
3. **The Authentication Server Function (AUSF):** This function is added in the home network. This decides whether an authentication request can be accepted or not. However, the authentication vector is created by UDM/ARPF.
4. **The Subscription Identifier De-concealing Function (SIDF):** This function decrypts the Subscription Concealed Identifier (SUCI), which is equivalent of GUCI used in 4G. The decryption of the SUCI gives the SUPI value. In the authentication protocols used in 5G, the SUPI value of an user is never transmitted over the network without encryption. The SUCI is created using public key cryptography, and only the SIDF is aware of the corresponding private key, while all the user equipment (UE) only gets the public key and creates the SUCI using the public key. This is the first prominent use of public key cryptography in any of the telecommunication security protocols.

There are three authentication protocols supported by 5G, namely 5G-AKA, EAP-AKA' and EAP-TLS. The 5G-AKA protocol is the direct replacement of the AKA protocol in 4G. The authentication procedure is similar to that of in 4G, with some differences due to the changes related to decisions that we have described and entry of new entities into the foray. The protocol is as follows.

1. The UE sends a signaling message to the SEAF using an assigned 5G-GUTI. If for some reason a GUTI has not been assigned to the UE, it sends the SUCI value.

2. The SEAF sends an authentication request to the AUSF in the home network that contains the UE, id, that is the 5G-GUTI or the SUCI value and the serving network (SN) name. The AUSF confirms the legitimacy of the serving network by confirming the SN name. Upon success, the AUSF forward the request to the UDM. If SUCI is sent, the UDM invokes the SIDF to get the SUPI value. The SUPI value contains the choice of the authentication protocol. In this case, 5G-AKA, and thus the protocol is then started by the UDM.
3. The UDM sends an authentication vector to the AUSF. The authentication vector is similar to the one used in the 4G-AKA protocol. It contains the following values.

   - The AUTN token which is used by the UE to authenticate the SN.
   - The XRES token which is used by the SN to authenticate the UE.
   - The K_{AUSF} token which contains the IK and CK values that are to be determined for the session.
   - The SUPI value if an SUCI value was sent by the UE.

   These methods are quite similar to 4G and therefore we do not further explain the process for obtaining each such token.
4. The AUSF stores the K_{AUSF} value and computes a hashed value of the expected response token, HXRES that is later matched with the response sent by the UE. It forward these values to the SEAF. It is to be noted that the SUPI value is forwarded to the SEAF only after the UE is authenticated.
5. The SEAF stores the HXRES value and forward the authentication vector to the UE.
6. The UE first authenticates the SN using the authentication token in a similar manner to that of the 4G-AKA protocol. Upon successful authentication, it creates the response token RES and sends it to the SEAF.
7. The SEAF uses the same hash on RES that it did on XRES and matches it. Upon successful matching, it sends it to the AUSF. The AUSF has the final decision about the confirmation of authentication. After that, the AUSF ensures that the AMF has the integrity and confidentiality keys in the following manner.
8. The AUSF creates K_{SEAF} and sends it to SEAF. The SEAF again modifies it and generates K_{AMF} which is sent to the AMF. The K_{AMF} contains the confidentiality and the integrity key which are needed for communication between UE and AMF. The UE had derived these values from the authentication token using the permanent secret keys, which results in both the UE and AMF having a shared pair of integrity and confidentiality keys.

As we can see, in this procedure the SUPI value is never transmitted without encryption and prior to the authentication at any stage. The final decisions about authentication is taken by the home network, giving the authentication protocol a more centralized view of control. The flowchart in Fig. 2.8 gives an overview of the protocol. In the flowchart, we omit some of the inner steps to make it simpler for understanding.

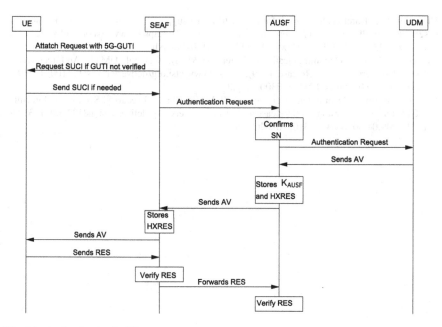

Fig. 2.8 Authentication in 5G

The ciphers used in the LTE architecture are the ones used for 5G as well. This is presumably because none of the ciphers are found to have any weakness that compromises their security in any way. For example, the ZUC cipher takes in 128-bit key and therefore can have at most 128-bit security. This is in fact the claimed security of the cipher as there has never been an attack that shows a key can be found in less than 2^{128} complexity. The 5G architecture also has an option to make the security of the system to 256-bit. In the case of ZUC, that only changes the method of key loading mechanism.

References

A Comparative Introduction to 4G and 5G Authentication. https://www.cablelabs.com/insights/a-comparative-introduction-to-4g-and-5g-authentication

A5/1 Decryption, https://opensource.srlabs.de/projects/a51-decrypt. Accessed Jan 2020

Briceno M, Goldberg I, Wagner D. An implementation of the GSM A3A8 algorithm. http://www.iol.ie/~kooltek/a3a8.txt. Last accessed in 2020

Digital cellular telecommunications system. General description of a GSM Public Land Mobile Network (PLMN). https://www.etsi.org/deliver/etsi_ts/101600_101699/101622/06.00.01_60/ts_101622v060001p.pdf

ETSI TS 133 501 V15.1.0 (2018-07). Security architecture and procedures for 5G System (3GPP TS 33.501 version 15.1.0 Release 15). https://www.etsi.org/deliver/etsi_ts/133500_133599/133501/15.01.00_60/ts_133501v150100p.pdf

LTE; Functional architecture and information flows to support mission critical communication services; (3GPP TS 23.1.179 version 13.4.0 Release 13). https://www.etsi.org/deliver/etsi_ts/123100_123199/123179/13.04.00_60/ts_123179v130400p.pdf

Universal Mobile Telecommunications System (UMTS). General UMTS Architecture(3G TS 23.101 version 3.0.1 Release 1999). https://www.etsi.org/deliver/etsi_ts/123100_123199/123101/03.00.01_60/ts_123101v030001p.pdf

Universal Mobile Telecommunications System (UMTS). LTE; 3G security; Security architecture (3GPP TS 33.102 version 9.4.0 Release 9). https://www.etsi.org/deliver/etsi_ts/133100_133199/133102/09.04.00_60/ts_133102v090400p.pdf

Chapter 3
Design Specification of ZUC Stream Cipher

Abstract In this chapter, we describe a detailed design specification of ZUC stream cipher. This cipher forms the core of the third set of integrity and confidentiality algorithm of the 4G LTE architecture. We describe the design specification of ZUC with respective C codes of different phases.

Keywords ZUC · S-box · Nonlinear function · LFSR

3.1 Structure of ZUC

ZUC (Specification of the 3GPP Confidentiality and Integrity Algorithms 128-EEA3 and 128-EIA3 2011a) is a word-based stream cipher which is the core component of the third standard of LTE. ZUC shares a very similar design architecture as SNOW 3G (Specification of the 3GPP Confidentiality and Integrity Algorithms UEA2 & UIA2 2006) and SNOW 2.0 (Ekdahl and Johansson 2002), in the sense that SNOW 3G and SNOW 2.0 are based on one LFSR, one finite state machine and one keystream generation function. ZUC is also LFSR-based and it has a nonlinear function which is similar to the finite state machine of SNOW 3G and SNOW 2.0. The registers of the finite state machines of SNOW 3G are updated by using S-boxes. For detailed design specification of SNOW 3G and SNOW 2.0, readers can look in to these articles (Specification of the 3GPP Confidentiality and Integrity Algorithms UEA2 & UIA2 2006; Ekdahl and Johansson 2002).

The ZUC (Specification of the 3GPP Confidentiality and Integrity Algorithms 128-EEA3 and 128-EIA3 2011a) has two phases, the first one being the key-IV initialization phase and the second one being keystream generation phase. In key-IV initialization phase, the state of the cipher will be initialized by n 128-bit secret key and a 128-bit initialization vector. During this phase, the Key Scheduling Algorithm will run for 32 rounds without generating any output. After this phase, the cipher enters into the keystream generation phase, here the cipher outputs 32 bits in every round. The design of ZUC stream cipher (Specification of the 3GPP Confidentiality and Integrity Algorithms 128-EEA3 and 128-EIA3 2011a) is based on the following three major components:

© The Author(s), under exclusive license to Springer Nature Singapore Pte Ltd. 2021   43
C. S. Mukherjee et al., *Design and Cryptanalysis of ZUC*,
SpringerBriefs on Cyber Security Systems and Networks,
https://doi.org/10.1007/978-981-33-4882-0_3

- One Linear Feedback Shift Register (LFSR),
- One Bit Reorganization Layer,
- One nonlinear function (F).

We first describe the structure of the cipher with the corresponding C-codes and then analyze different properties of the cipher in a later chapter. The C-codes that are described in this chapter are based on what is explained in Specification of the 3GPP Confidentiality and Integrity Algorithms 128-EEA3 and 128-EIA3 (2011a).

3.1.1 Linear Feedback Shift Register of ZUC

The LFSR of ZUC is built differently than most of the other stream ciphers. The LFSRs of most of the stream ciphers are built on some extension of $GF(2)$. However, the LFSR in ZUC is built on $GF(2^{31} - 1)$. The elements of this field (i.e., $GF(2^{31} - 1)$) are $\{1, 2, \ldots, 2^{31} - 1\}$. This implies that the zero element is represented by $2^{31} - 1$. The operations in this field are same as modular arithmetic, only that the zero element is represented in a different way. The LFSR of ZUC is a 16-word register, i.e., if $S = (s_0, \ldots, s_{15})$ is a state of the LFSR then each s_i's will be of 31-bit. As the LFSR is a 16-word register, so the maximum periodicity can be $(2^{31} - 1)^{16} \approx 2^{496}$. From our discussion in Chap. 1, we know that an LFSR can achieve the maximum period if a primitive polynomial is used for forming the linear feedback function. ZUC uses one such primitive polynomial $f(x)$ over $GF(2^{31} - 1)$, where

$$f(x) = x^{16} - \left(2^{15}x^{15} + 2^{17}x^{13} + 2^{21}x^{10} + 2^{20}x^4 + (2^8 + 1)\right).$$

Hence, the feedback function of the LFSR is

$$s_{15}^{t+1} = 2^{15}s_{15}^t + 2^{17}s_{13}^t + 2^{21}s_{10}^t + 2^{20}s_4^t + (2^8 + 1)s_0^t,$$

where $s_0^t, s_1^t, \ldots, s_{15}^t$ are the state words of tth clock. The state update function of the LFSR will be as follows:

---

1. $s_i^{t+1} = s_{i+1}^t$ for $0 \leq i \leq 14$,
2. $s_{15}^{t+1} = 2^{15}s_{15}^t + 2^{17}s_{13}^t + 2^{21}s_{10}^t + 2^{20}s_4^t + (2^8 + 1)s_0^t$.

This is the algorithmic implementation of the state update function that derives the $(t + 1)$th state from the tth state of the LFSR. However, during the key scheduling phase, the feedback of the LFSR also contains a modified output from the nonlinear function F. But during the keystream generation phase, the output from the nonlinear function F is not masked with the feedback function of the LFSR. We also describe detailed algorithmic representation of these phases with the code snippets in the respective sections.

The addition and multiplications used here are under modulo $2^{31} - 1$, with the value 0 replaced with $2^{31} - 1$. As we can see, the feedback of the LFSR requires elements in some of the states of the LFSR to be multiplied by a power of 2. This multiplication of x by 2^k can be computed by simply left rotating x by k bits. Suppose $a = a_{31}a_{30} \cdots a_0$, where $a_i \in GF(2)$ and $b = 2^k a$ then $b = b_{31}b_{30} \cdots b_0$, where $b_{i+k} = a_i \ \forall i : i + k \leq 31$ as

$$a = a_{31}2^{31} + a_{30}2^{30} + \cdots + a_0$$
$$b = a2^k = a_{31}2^{31+k} + a_{30}2^{30+k} \cdots + a_0 2^k.$$

If $i + k = 31 + j$, where $(1 \leq j \leq 31)$ then we need to find the representative elements of 2^{i+k} in this corresponding finite field.

$$2^{i+k} = 2^{31+j} \mod (2^{31} - 1)$$
$$= (2^{31} - 1)2^j + 2^j \mod (2^{31} - 1)$$
$$= 2^j.$$

This implies that multiplying an element a by 2^k can be done by left rotating a by k bits.

3.1.2 Bit Reorganization Layer of ZUC

The bit reorganization layer consists of four 32 bit registers, namely X_0, X_1, X_2, X_3. Each of these registers are formed by mixing 16 bits from two states of the LFSR. Below we write the expressions of each of these registers:

- $X_0 = s_{15H} \| s_{14L}$,
- $X_1 = s_{11L} \| s_{9H}$,
- $X_2 = s_{7L} \| s_{5H}$,
- $X_3 = s_{2L} \| s_{0H}$.

The corresponding code-snippet of bit reorganization layer is provided in Code 3.1.

```
1  void BitReorganization()
2  {
3       X_0 = ((LFSR_S15 & 0x7FFF8000) << 1) | (LFSR_S14
         & 0xFFFF);
4       X_1 = ((LFSR_S11 & 0xFFFF) << 16) | (LFSR_S9 >>
         15);
5       X_2 = ((LFSR_S7 & 0xFFFF) << 16) | (LFSR_S5 >>
         15);
6       X_3 = ((LFSR_S2 & 0xFFFF) << 16) | (LFSR_S0 >>
         15);
7  }
```

Code 3.1 Code-snippet of bit reorganization layer

3.1.3 Nonlinear Function of ZUC (F)

The nonlinear function of ZUC consists of the following three components:

- Two 32-bit registers, namely R_1 and R_2.
- Two linear transformation functions $\mathcal{L}_1$ and $\mathcal{L}_2$.
- Two S-boxes, $S_0 : \{0, 1\}^8 \to \{0, 1\}^8$ and $S_1 : \{0, 1\}^8 \to \{0, 1\}^8$.

We describe each of these parts in detail. We start by describing the linear transformation functions $\mathcal{L}_1$ and $\mathcal{L}_2$. These two linear transformations takes 32-bit inputs and produce 32-bit outputs, and are invertible in case of ZUC. The algebraic structure of $\mathcal{L}_1$ and $\mathcal{L}_2$ are provided in Eqs. (3.1) and (3.2).

$$\mathcal{L}_1(X) = X \oplus (X \lll_{32} 2) \oplus (X \lll_{32} 10) \oplus (X \lll_{32} 18) \oplus (X \lll_{32} 24). \quad (3.1)$$
$$\mathcal{L}_2(X) = X \oplus (X \lll_{32} 8) \oplus (X \lll_{32} 14) \oplus (X \lll_{32} 22) \oplus (X \lll_{32} 30). \quad (3.2)$$

The function F uses two Substitution Boxes $S_0 : \{0, 1\}^8 \to \{0, 1\}^8$ and $S_1 : \{0, 1\}^8 \to \{0, 1\}^8$. The description of the S-boxes S_0 and S_1 are described in the Tables 3.1 and 3.2 respectively.

The function F uses a combination of these two S-boxes S_0 and S_1 to form a function S whose input size and output size are 32 bits. The algebraic structure of S is described in Eq. (3.3):

Table 3.1 The S-box S_0

	00	01	02	03	04	05	06	07	08	09	0A	0B	0C	0D	0E	0F
00	3E	72	5B	47	CA	E0	00	33	04	D1	54	98	09	B9	6D	CB
01	7B	1B	F9	32	AF	9D	6A	A5	B8	2D	FC	1D	08	53	03	90
02	4D	4E	84	99	E4	CE	D9	91	DD	B6	85	48	8B	29	6E	AC
03	CD	C1	F8	1E	73	43	69	C6	B5	BD	FD	39	63	20	D4	38
04	76	7D	B2	A7	CF	ED	57	C5	F3	2C	BB	14	21	06	55	9B
05	E3	EF	5E	31	4F	7F	5A	A4	0D	82	51	49	5F	BA	58	1C
06	4A	16	D5	17	A8	92	24	1F	8C	FF	D8	AE	2E	01	D3	AD
07	3B	4B	DA	46	EB	C9	DE	9A	8F	87	D7	3A	80	6F	2F	C8
08	B1	B4	37	F7	0A	22	13	28	7C	CC	3C	89	C7	C3	96	56
09	07	BF	7E	F0	0B	2B	97	52	35	41	79	61	A6	4C	10	FE
0A	BC	26	95	88	8A	B0	A3	FB	C0	18	94	F2	E1	E5	E9	5D
0B	D0	DC	11	66	64	5C	EC	59	42	75	12	F5	74	9C	AA	23
0C	0E	86	AB	BE	2A	02	E7	67	E6	44	A2	6C	C2	93	9F	F1
0D	F6	FA	36	D2	50	68	9E	62	71	15	3D	D6	40	C4	E2	0F
0E	8E	83	77	6B	25	05	3F	0C	30	EA	70	B7	A1	E8	A9	65
0F	8D	27	1A	DB	81	B3	A0	F4	45	7A	19	DF	EE	78	34	60

Table 3.2 The S-box S_1

	0	1	2	3	4	5	6	7	8	9	0A	0B	0C	0D	0E	0F
0	55	C2	63	71	3B	C8	47	86	9F	3X	DA	5B	29	AA	FD	77
1	8C	C5	94	0C	A6	1A	13	00	E3	A8	16	72	40	F9	F8	42
2	44	26	68	96	81	D9	45	3E	10	76	C6	A7	8B	39	43	E1
3	3A	B5	56	2A	C0	6D	B3	05	22	66	BF	DC	0B	FA	62	48
4	DD	20	11	06	36	C9	C1	Cf	F6	27	52	BB	69	F5	D4	87
5	7F	84	4C	d2	9C	57	A4	BC	4F	9A	DF	FE	D6	8D	7A	EB
6	2B	53	D8	5C	A1	14	17	FB	23	D5	7D	30	67	73	08	09
7	EE	B7	70	3F	61	B2	19	8E	4E	E5	4B	93	8F	5D	DB	A9
8	AD	F1	AE	2E	CB	0D	FC	F4	2D	46	6E	1D	97	E8	D1	E9
9	4D	37	A5	75	5E	83	9E	AB	82	9D	B9	1C	E0	CD	49	89
0A	01	B6	BD	58	24	A2	5F	38	78	99	15	90	50	B8	95	E4
0B	D0	91	C7	CE	ED	0F	B4	6F	A0	CC	F0	02	4A	79	C3	DE
0C	A3	EF	EA	51	E6	6B	18	EC	1B	2C	80	F7	74	E7	FF	21
0D	5A	6A	54	1E	41	31	92	35	C4	33	07	0A	BA	7E	0E	34
0E	88	B1	98	7C	F3	3D	60	6C	7B	CA	D3	1f	32	65	04	28
0F	64	BE	85	9B	2F	59	8A	D7	B0	25	AC	AF	12	03	E2	F2

$$S(\mathbf{x}) = S_0(\mathbf{x} \gg 24) \parallel S_1(\mathbf{x} \gg 16 \wedge \texttt{0xFF}) \parallel S_0(\mathbf{x} \gg 8 \wedge \texttt{0xFF}) \parallel S_1(\mathbf{x} \wedge \texttt{0xFF}).$$
(3.3)

As evident from the definition of S (Eq. (3.3)), the most significant 8 bits are used as inputs to S_0, the next 8 bits are used as inputs to S_1, and again the next 8 bits are used as inputs to S_0 and the least significant 8 bits are fed to S_1. The outputs are concatenated in that order. A simple function merge32 is used for the concatenation. Having discussed the components of F, now we write the pseudo-code of F in Algorithm 3.1 and describe its operations.

Algorithm 3.1: The nonlinear function F

---

1 **Input:** (X_0, X_1, X_2);
2 **Output:** W;
3 $W \leftarrow (X_0 \oplus R_1) \boxplus R_2$;
4 $W_1 \leftarrow R_1 \boxplus X_1$;
5 $W_2 \leftarrow R_2 \oplus X_2$;
6 $R_1 \leftarrow S\big(L_1(W_{1L} \parallel W_{2H})\big)$;
7 $R_2 \leftarrow S\big(L_2(W_{2L} \parallel W_{1H})\big)$;

The corresponding C code of nonlinear function F is provided in Code 3.2. From here on, we use u32 to denote the unsigned integer data type uint32_t.

```
1 #define merge32(a, b, c, d) (((u32)(a) << 24) |
2 ((u32)(b) << 16) | ((u32)(c) << 8) | ((u32)(d)))
3 u32 F(){
4     u32 W, W1, W2, u, v;
```

```
5      W = (X_0 ^ F_R1) + F_R2;
6      W1 = F_R1 + X_1; W2 = F_R2 ^ X_2;
7      u = L1((W1 << 16) | (W2 >> 16));
8      v = L2((W2 << 16) | (W1 >> 16));
9      F_R1 = merge32(S0[u >> 24], S1[(u >> 16) & 0xFF],
10     S0[(u >> 8) & 0xFF], S1[u & 0xFF]);
11     F_R2 = merge32(S0[v >> 24], S1[(v >> 16) & 0xFF],
12     S0[(v >> 8) & 0xFF], S1[v & 0xFF]);
13     return W;
14 }
```

Code 3.2 Nonlinear function (F)

3.2 Working Principle of ZUC 1.4

In this section, we provide a detailed working principle of ZUC 1.4. As we know the cipher is based on two phases. In the key-IV initialization phase, the cipher will be initialized by a 128-bit key K and a 128-bit initialization vector IV. As we know, the ZUC is based on a register with 496 bits. Among these 496 bits, 256 bits will be initialized by key and IV and remaining 240 bits will be initialized to some padding bits. These 240 padding bits are constant and are defined as 16 15-bit constants. They are represented as $d_0, d_1, \ldots, d_{15}$. We represent the key (K) as $K = k_{15} \parallel k_{14} \parallel \cdots \parallel k_0$ and the initialization vector (IV) as $IV = iv_{15} \parallel iv_{14} \parallel \cdots \parallel iv_0$, where each k_i and iv_i are 8 bit values. The exact values of padding bits are described below.

$$d_0 = 100010011010111_2 = 0x44D7_{16}, \quad d_1 = 010011010111100_2 = 0x26BC_{16},$$
$$d_2 = 110001001101011_2 = 0x626B_{16}, \quad d_3 = 001001101011110_2 = 0x135E_{16},$$
$$d_4 = 101011110001001_2 = 0x5789_{16}, \quad d_5 = 011010111100010_2 = 0x35E2_{16},$$
$$d_6 = 111000100110101_2 = 0x7135_{16}, \quad d_7 = 000100110101111_2 = 0x09AF_{16},$$
$$d_8 = 100110101111000_2 = 0x4D78_{16}, \quad d_9 = 010111100010011_2 = 0x2F13_{16},$$
$$d_{10} = 110101111000100_2 = 0x6BC4_{16}, \quad d_{11} = 001101011110001_2 = 0x1AF1_{16},$$
$$d_{12} = 101111000100110_2 = 0x5E26_{16}, \quad d_{13} = 011110001001101_2 = 0x3C4D_{16},$$
$$d_{14} = 111100010011010_2 = 0x789A_{16}, \quad d_{15} = 100011110101100_2 = 0x47AC_{16}.$$

We start by calling the initialization function which takes a key and IV as input to initialize the state of the cipher ZUC.

```
1  Initialization(key,IV);
2  /* here key and IV are two arrays with 16 blocks
3     that hold 8 bit values each*/
```

First, the state of LFSR will be initialized as $s_i = k_i||d_i||iv_i$, $i = 0, \ldots, 15$, and the registers R_1 and R_2 will be initialized to 0. The code of the initialization function is provided in Code 3.3.

```
1  #define merge31(a,b,c)  (((u32)(a)>> 23)|((u32)(b)>>8)
      |(u32)(c))
2
3  void Initialization(u32* k,  u32* iv)
4  {
5      u32 w, nCount;
6      /* expand key */
7      LFSR_S0  =  merge31(k[0],  d[0],  iv[0]);
8      LFSR_S1  =  merge31(k[1],  d[1],  iv[1]);
9      LFSR_S2  =  merge31(k[2],  d[2],  iv[2]);
10     LFSR_S3  =  merge31(k[3],  d[3],  iv[3]);
11     LFSR_S4  =  merge31(k[4],  d[4],  iv[4]);
12     LFSR_S5  =  merge31(k[5],  d[5],  iv[5]);
13     LFSR_S6  =  merge31(k[6],  d[6],  iv[6]);
14     LFSR_S7  =  merge31(k[7],  d[7],  iv[7]);
15     LFSR_S8  =  merge31(k[8],  d[8],  iv[8]);
16     LFSR_S9  =  merge31(k[9],  d[9],  iv[9]);
17     LFSR_S10 =  merge31(k[10],d[10],  iv[10]);
18     LFSR_S11 =  merge31(k[11],d[11],  iv[11]);
19     LFSR_S12 =  merge31(k[12],d[12],  iv[12]);
20     LFSR_S13 =  merge31(k[13],d[13],  iv[13]);
21     LFSR_S14 =  merge31(k[14],d[14],  iv[14]);
22     LFSR_S15 =  merge31(k[15],d[15],  iv[15]);
23     /* set F_R1 and F_R2 to zero */
24     F_R1  =  0;
25     F_R2  =  0;
26 }
```

Code 3.3 Initialization function

After that, the cipher will be clocked 32 times in the initialization mode. The values of X_0, X_1, X_2 and X_3 are calculated at each step by using `BitReorganization` function (see Sect. 3.1.2). During this, the cipher will not produce any output rather the output from the nonlinear function is masked with the feedback of the LFSR. This completes the initialization phase of the LFSR. In Code 3.4, we provide the key scheduling phase of ZUC.

```
1  nCount = 32;
2  while (nCount > 0)
3  {
4      BitReorganization();
5      w=F()^X_3;
6
```

```
7        LFSRimode (w >> 1) ;
8        nCount --;
9 }
```

Code 3.4 Key scheduling process

In the Code 3.5, we provide the code of the function LFSRimode which is used in Code 3.4.

```
1 void LFSRimode (u32 u)
2 {
3        u32 f, v;
4        f = LFSR_S0;
5        v = MulByPow2 (LFSR_S0 , 8) ;
6        f = AddM (f, v) ;
7        v = MulByPow2 (LFSR_S4 , 20) ;
8        f = AddM (f, v) ;
9        v = MulByPow2 (LFSR_S10 , 21) ;
10       f = AddM (f, v) ;
11       v = MulByPow2 (LFSR_S13 , 17) ;
12       f = AddM (f, v) ;
13       v = MulByPow2 (LFSR_S15 , 15) ;
14       f = AddM (f, v) ;
15
16       if (f==0)
17          f=0x7fffffff;
18       f=f^u;
19       if (f==0)
20          f=0x7fffffff;
21
22       /* update the state */
23       LFSR_S0 = LFSR_S1;LFSR_S1 = LFSR_S2;
24       LFSR_S2 = LFSR_S3;LFSR_S3 = LFSR_S4;
25       LFSR_S4 = LFSR_S5;LFSR_S5 = LFSR_S6;
26       LFSR_S6 = LFSR_S7;LFSR_S7 = LFSR_S8;
27       LFSR_S8 = LFSR_S9;LFSR_S9 = LFSR_S10;
28       LFSR_S10 = LFSR_S11;LFSR_S11 = LFSR_S12;
29       LFSR_S12 = LFSR_S13;LFSR_S13 = LFSR_S14;
30       LFSR_S14 = LFSR_S15;LFSR_S15 = f;
31 }
```

Code 3.5 State update function during key scheduling phase

Algorithm 3.2 explains the algorithm for clocking of LFSR in the initialization mode.

Algorithm 3.2: LFSR in Initialization Mode

---

1 **Input:** $s_0, s_1, \ldots s_{15}, u$ $\triangleright (u = w \oplus X_3) \gg 1$, where w is the output of F (see Algorithm 3.1) ;

2 $v \leftarrow (2^{15} s_{15} + 2^{17} s_{13} + 2^{21} s_{10} + 2^{20} s_4 + (1 + 2^8) s_0) \mod (2^{31} - 1)$;

3 $v \leftarrow (v \oplus u) \mod (2^{31} - 1)$;

4 **if** $v = 0$ **then**

5 | $v \leftarrow 2^{31} - 1;$

6 **end**

7 **for** $i = 0$ *to* 15 **do**

8 | $s_i \leftarrow s_{i+1};$

9 **end**

This terminates the initialization process of the ZUC stream cipher. After this, the cipher starts generating keystreams. For generation of keystream, a separate function is called, which is called `GenStream(u32 c1,int d)`.

```
1  GenStream(c1,d);
2  /* Here, c1 is an array in which the generated
      keystreams
3     are going to be stored
4     d is the number of 32-bit keystream words that
      need to be
5     generated.
6  */
```

At first, the LFSR is clocked once, but the output of F is discarded. After that, the cipher enters into a mode, which is known as working mode. The LFSR will be clocked in working mode for d rounds. In each round, the function generates a 32-bit keystream word. The procedure described in Code 3.6 is followed to generate keystream word.

```
1  void GenStream(u32* pKeystream, int Length)
2  {
3       int i;
4       BitReorganization();
5       F();
6       LFSRWithWorkMode();
7
8       /* The output of F is discarded once at the
         beginning
9            It is important to note that the
         BitReorganization()
10           function is invoked at each round
11      */
12
13      for (i = 0; i < Length; i ++)
14      {
15           BitReorganization();
16           pKeystream[i] = F() ^ X_3;
```

```
17        /*
18           The output of F is XOR'ed with the X_3
19           variable and stored as the key stream
20        */

22           LFSRWorkMode();
23        }
24 }
```

Code 3.6 Keystream generation process

The function `LFSRWorkMode()` used in Code 3.6 is described in Code 3.7.

```
 1 void LFSRWorkMode()
 2 {
 3      u32 f, v;
 4      f = LFSR_S0;
 5      v = MulByPow2(LFSR_S0, 8);
 6      f = AddM(f, v);
 7      v = MulByPow2(LFSR_S4, 20);
 8      f = AddM(f, v);
 9      v = MulByPow2(LFSR_S10, 21);
10      f = AddM(f, v);
11      v = MulByPow2(LFSR_S13, 17);
12      f = AddM(f, v);
13      v = MulByPow2(LFSR_S15, 15);
14      f = AddM(f, v);
15      /* update the state */
16      LFSR_S0 =LFSR_S1;LFSR_S1 =LFSR_S2;
17      LFSR_S2 =LFSR_S3;LFSR_S3 =LFSR_S4;
18      LFSR_S4 = LFSR_S5;LFSR_S5 = LFSR_S6;
19      LFSR_S6 = LFSR_S7;LFSR_S7 = LFSR_S8;
20      LFSR_S8 = LFSR_S9;LFSR_S9 = LFSR_S10;
21      LFSR_S10 = LFSR_S11;LFSR_S11 = LFSR_S12;
22      LFSR_S12 = LFSR_S13;LFSR_S13 = LFSR_S14;
23      LFSR_S14 = LFSR_S15;LFSR_S15 = f;
24 }
```

Code 3.7 LFSRWorkMode function

Now we look into the functioning of the LFSR in the working mode to get a complete idea about the working procedure. The working procedure is described in Algorithm 3.3.

We provide a complete pictorial view of initialization and keystream generation procedure of ZUC in Figs. 3.1 and 3.2 respectively.

This version of ZUC had some weakness that was pointed out by Wu et al. (2012) which led to some modifications in the design specification of ZUC. We describe the attack in Chap. 5. The updated cipher which prevents the attack of Wu et al. (2012) is known as ZUC 1.6. In Sect. 3.3, we point out the differences between ZUC 1.4 and ZUC 1.6.

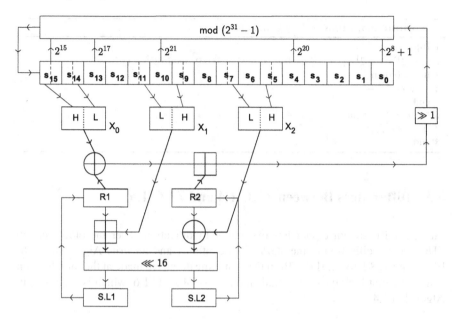

Fig. 3.1 Initialization phase of ZUC

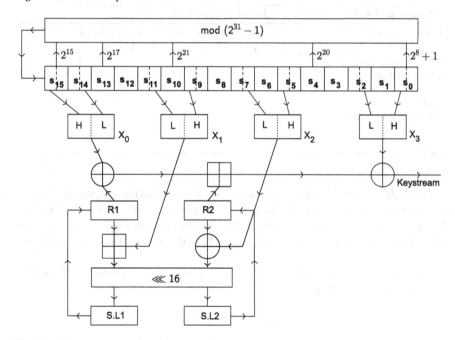

Fig. 3.2 Keystream generation phase of ZUC

Algorithm 3.3: LFSR in Key generation Mode

---

1 **Input:** $s_0, s_1, \ldots, s_{15}$;
2 $v = (2^{15}s_{15} + 2^{17}s_{13} + 2^{21}s_{10} + 2^{20}s_4 + (1 + 2^8)s_0) \mod (2^{31} - 1)$;
3 **if** $v = 0$ **then**
4 $\quad | \quad v \leftarrow 2^{31} - 1$;
5 **end**
6 **for** $i = 0$ *to* 15 **do**
7 $\quad | \quad s_i \leftarrow s_{i+1}$;
8 **end**

3.3   Differences Between ZUC 1.4 and ZUC 1.6

The ZUC 1.6 stream cipher has two major modifications over the older version ZUC 1.4 (Specification of the 3GPP Confidentiality and Integrity Algorithms 128-EEA3 and 128-EIA3 2011b). Both these modifications are made at the initialization phase. We first look into the initialization phase of ZUC 1.6, which is described in Algorithm 3.4.

Algorithm 3.4: Initialization Mode of LFSR in ZUC 1.6

---

1 **Input:** $s_0, s_1, \ldots, s_{15}, u$ ▷ Here $u = w \gg 1$ where w is the output of F;
2 $v = (2^{15}s_{15} + 2^{17}s_{13} + 2^{21}s_{10} + 2^{20}s_4 + (1 + 2^8)s_0) \mod (2^{31} - 1)$;
3 $v = (v + u) \mod (2^{31} - 1)$;
4 **if** $v = 0$ **then**
5 $\quad | \quad v \leftarrow 2^{31} - 1$;
6 **end**
7 **for** $i = 0$ *to* 15 **do**
8 $\quad | \quad s_i \leftarrow s_{i+1}$;
9 **end**

From Algorithms 3.2 and 3.4, one can easily observed that the assignment of s_{16} in the second step has been updated from $s_{16} = (u \oplus v)$ to $s_{16} = (v + u) \mod (2^{31} - 1)$. Here, s_i are the state words of the LFSR. The other change made is that here $u = W \gg 1$ instead of $u = W \oplus X_3 \gg 1$, where W is the output of nonlinear function F.

Below we provide the codes of initialization phase of ZUC 1.4 and ZUC 1.6 and point out the specific differences.

```
1                 /* ZUC 1.4 */
2    void LFSRimode(u32 u)
3    {
4          u32 f, v;
5          f = LFSR_S0;
6          v = MulByPow2(LFSR_S0, 8);
7          f = AddM(f, v);
8          v = MulByPow2(LFSR_S4, 20)
      ;
9          f = AddM(f, v);
10         v = MulByPow2(LFSR_S10,
      21);
11         f = AddM(f, v);
12         v = MulByPow2(LFSR_S13,
      17);
13         f = AddM(f, v);
14         v = MulByPow2(LFSR_S15,
      15);
15         f = AddM(f, v);
16         /* ZUC 1.4 */
17         if(f==0)
18             f=0x7fffffff;
19         f=f^u;
20         if(f==0)
21             f=0x7fffffff;
22   }
23
```

```
1                  /* ZUC 1.6 */
2
3    void LFSRimode(u32 u)
4    {
5          u32 f, v;
6          f = LFSR_S0;
7          v = MulByPow2(LFSR_S0,
      8);
8          f = AddM(f, v);
9          v = MulByPow2(LFSR_S4,
      20);
10         f = AddM(f, v);
11         v = MulByPow2(LFSR_S10,
      21);
12         f = AddM(f, v);
13         v = MulByPow2(LFSR_S13,
      17);
14         f = AddM(f, v);
15         v = MulByPow2(LFSR_S15,
      15);
16         f = AddM(f, v);
17         f= AddM(f, u); //ZUC
      1.6
18   }
```

```
1              /*ZUC 1.4 */
2    while (nCount > 0)
3    {
4          BitReorganization();
5          w=F()^BRC_X3;//ZUC 1.4
6          LFSRimode(w >> 1);
7          nCount --;
8    }
9
```

```
1               /* ZUC 1.6 */
2    while (nCount > 0)
3    {
4          BitReorganization();
5          w = F();//ZUC 1.6
6          LFSRimode(w >> 1);
7          nCount --;
8    }
9
```

In Appendix A, we have provided a few test vectors to verify the implementation of ZUC 1.4 and ZUC 1.6. For ZUC 1.6, one may also refer to ZUC Stream Cipher (2020).

3.4   Confidentiality Algorithm Using ZUC

The confidentiality algorithm of the third standard of LTE (i.e., 128-EEA3) ETSI/SAGE Specification (2011) is based on symmetric key primitive. It is based on the stream cipher ZUC. It uses symmetric key CK to encrypt the data. The block of data may be of size 1 to 2^{32} bits long. The confidentiality algorithm 128-EEA3 (ETSI/SAGE Specification 2011) takes the following inputs, which are described in Table 3.3.

Table 3.3 Input to the confidentiality algorithm 128-EEA3

Input	Size (in bits)	Type
$COUNT$	32	The counter
$BEARER$	5	The bearer identity
$DIRECTION$	1	The direction of transmission
CK	128	The confidential key
$LENGTH$	32	The length of the message
M	$LENGTH$	The message

Table 3.4 Output from the confidentiality algorithm 128-EEA3

Output	Size (in bits)	Type
C	$LENGTH$	The ciphertext

The detail of the output from the confidentiality algorithm 128-EEA3 is described in Table 3.4.

The confidentiality algorithm 128-EEA3 is based on three phases. The first phase is initialization phase, where the parameters of ZUC are initialized by key and initialization vectors. The next phase is keystream bit generation phase, where the cipher generates keystream bits. In the third phase, these generated keystream bits are used to encrypt (similarly to decrypt) the message (similarly the ciphertext) for encryption (decryption). Below we provide a detailed description of these phases.

3.4.1 Initialization Phase

In this section, we describe the initialization phase of the confidentiality algorithm 128-EEA3. During this phase, the key of the stream cipher ZUC will be initialized by confidential key CK and the IV will be initialized by $COUNTER, BEARER, DIRECTION$. Let $CK[i]$ denotes the ith confidential byte of the confidential key CK and $KEY[i]$ denotes the ith byte of the 128-bit key of stream cipher ZUC.

$$CK = CK[0] \parallel CK[1] \parallel \cdots \parallel CK[15]$$
$$KEY = KEY[0] \parallel KEY[1] \parallel \cdots \parallel KEY[15].$$

$COUNT[i]$ denotes the ith byte of 32-bit counter $COUNT$.

$$COUNT = COUNT[0] \parallel COUNT[1] \parallel \cdots \parallel COUNT[3].$$

Each byte of 128-bit initialization vector IV is denoted by $IV[i], 0 \le i \le 15$.

$$IV = IV[0] \parallel IV[1] \parallel \cdots \parallel IV[15].$$

The Algorithm 3.5 to initialize key and IV of ZUC.

Algorithm 3.5: Initialization Algorithm of 128-EEA3

---

1 $KEY[i] = CK[i]\ 0 \le i \le 15$;
2 $IV[i] = COUNT[i]\ 0 \le i \le 3$;
3 $IV[4] = BEARER \parallel DIRECTION \parallel 00_2$;
4 $IV[5] = IV[6] = IV[7] = 00000000_2$;
5 $IV[8] = IV[0],\ IV[9] = IV[1]$;
6 $IV[10] = IV[2],\ IV[11] = IV[3]$;
7 $IV[12] = IV[4],\ IV[13] = IV[5]$;
8 $IV[14] = IV[6],\ IV[15] = IV[7]$.

3.4.2 Keystream Generation Phase

In this phase, the ZUC stream cipher generates keystream words of length L. Further, each word is expanded into bit strings of length 32. Let $z[0], z[1], \ldots, z[32 \times L - 1]$ be the expanded keystream bits. Then $z[0]$ and $z[31]$ are the most significant bit and the least significant bit of the first output word respectively. These keystream bits are used to encrypt/decrypt a message/ciphertext of same length as the length of generated keystream bits. If the length of the message/ciphertext is $LENGTH$, then $LENGTH = L \times 32$.

3.4.3 Encryption/Decryption Phase

In this, phase the message/ciphertext bits are encrypted/decrypted by using generated keystream bits. Let M be the message of length $LENGTH$ and $M[i]$ denotes the ith bit of the message, i.e., $M = M[0] \parallel M[1] \parallel \cdots \parallel M[LENGTH - 1]$. Let the corresponding ciphertext be C and $C[i]$ be the ith ciphertext bit, i.e., $C = C[0] \parallel C[1] \parallel \cdots \parallel C[LENGTH - 1]$. The encryption technique which is used to generate these ciphertext bits is

$$C[i] = M[i] \oplus z[i],\ 0 \le i \le LENGTH - 1.$$

Similarly, the decryption process will be,

Table 3.5 Input to the integrity algorithm 128-EIA3

Input	Size (in bits)	Type
$COUNT$	32	The counter
$BEARER$	5	The bearer identity
$DIRECTION$	1	The direction of transmission
IK	128	The integrity key
$LENGTH$	32	The length of the message
M	$LENGTH$	The message

Table 3.6 Output from the integrity algorithm 128-EIA3

Output	Size (in bits)	Type
MAC	32	The message authentication code

$$M[i] = C[i] \oplus z[i], \ 0 \leq i \leq LENGTH - 1.$$

3.5   Integrity Algorithm

The integrity algorithm of 3GPP is known as 128-EIA3 (ETSI/SAGE Specification 2011). This is based on message authentication code (MAC) function. The MAC function is used to compute the message authentication code of a message by using a key. This key is known as the integrity key and it is denoted by IK. The length of the message on which the message authentication code needs to be generated can be of length 1 to 65504 bits.

The inputs and the output of 128-EIA3 algorithm are described in Tables 3.5 and 3.6 respectively.

The integrity algorithm 128-EIA3 (ETSI/SAGE Specification 2011) is based on three phases. The first phase is known as initialization phase, where the key and initialization vector are initialized by the integrity key and other parameters. The next phase is known as keystream generation phase, where the keystream bits will be generated. These generated keystream bits are used to generate message authentication code in the final phase of 128-EIA3.

3.5.1   Initialization Phase

In this section, we describe the initialization phase of integrity algorithm 128-EIA3. Let IK be the 128-bit integrity key and $IK[i]$ be the ith byte of IK, i.e., $IK =$

$IK[0] \parallel IK[2] \parallel \cdots \parallel IK[15]$. Let KEY be the initial 128-bit key of ZUC stream cipher and $KEY[i]$ be the ith byte of KEY, i.e., $KEY = KEY[0] \parallel KEY[2] \parallel \cdots \parallel KEY[15]$. Let $COUNT[i]$ be the ith byte of the 32-bit counter $COUNT$ and $IV[i]$ denote the ith byte of the 128-bit initialization vector IV, i.e.,

$$COUNT = COUNT[0] \parallel COUNT[1] \parallel \cdots \parallel COUNT[3]$$
$$IV = IV[0] \parallel IV[1] \parallel \cdots \parallel IV[15].$$

Algorithm 3.6 will be followed to initialize the key and initialization vector of ZUC stream cipher. One can see that the inputs in the initialization phase for both the confidentiality and the integrity algorithms are same. However, the way they are loaded in to the initialization vector is different.

Algorithm 3.6: Initialization Algorithm of 128-EIA3

1 $KEY[i] = IK[i]$ $0 \le i \le 15$;
2 $IV[i] = COUNT[i]$ $0 \le i \le 3$;
3 $IV[4] = BEARER \parallel 000_2$;
4 $IV[5] = IV[6] = IV[7] = 00000000_2$;
5 $IV[8] = IV[0] + (DIRECTION \ll 7)$;
6 $IV[9] = IV[1]$;
7 $IV[10] = IV[2]$, $IV[11] = IV[3]$;
8 $IV[12] = IV[4]$, $IV[13] = IV[5]$;
9 $IV[14] = IV[6] \oplus (DIRECTION \ll 7)$;
10 $IV[15] = IV[7]$.

3.5.2 Keystream Generation Phase

In this phase, the ZUC stream cipher generates the keystreams after performing the initialization phase. The number of keystream words generated is equal to $L = \lceil \frac{LENGTH}{32} \rceil + 2$. Further, these keystream words are expanded into bits and these bits are denoted by $z[0]$, $z[1]$, $\cdots$, $z[32 \times L - 1]$. The indexing is same as in the confidentiality algorithm. For this algorithm, we denote the bit string $z[i]z[i+1] \ldots z[i+31]$ by z_i. These keystream bits are used to generate message authentication code corresponding to the message to be encrypted.

3.5.3 Generation of MAC

This is the final phase of 128-EIA3, where the message authentication code (MAC) is generated. The Algorithm 3.7 is used to generate the message authentication code corresponding to message M. It is important to note that the MAC is generated corresponding to the plaintext prior to its encryption.

Algorithm 3.7: MAC of 128-EIA3

---

1 Set $T = 0$;
  /* Here T is a 32-bit word   */
2 For each $i = 0, \dots, LENGTH - 1$ if $M[i] = 1$, then $T = T \oplus z_i$;
3 Set $T = T \oplus z_{LENGTH}$;
4 $MAC = T \oplus z_{32 \times (L-1)}$.

As we can see from the algorithm the generated keystream is added into an accumulator 32-bit at a time depending on the different message bits. At first, a 32-bit accumulator is initialized to 0. Then a sliding window mechanism is used which runs for rounds equal to the length of the message. In the ith round keystream, z_i is bitwise XOR'ed to the accumulator if the ith bit of the message, $M[i]$ is 1. After this loop terminates, the keystream z_{LENGTH} is XOR'ed to the accumulator indifferent of the message. At last, the keystream word $z_{32 \times (L-1)}$ is also XOR'ed with the accumulator. The resultant 32-bit string in the accumulator is the final MAC which is sent as the verifier for the integrity of the message. This is exactly the methodology that we have discussed in Sect. 1.7 of Chap. 1.

3.6   Description of ZUC-256

As we have already discussed, the 5G architecture currently operates on 128-bit security provided by a 128-bit key. However, there is an option for increasing the security of the architecture to 256 bit, and for that, the ciphers need to be initialized with 256-bit key (The ZUC-256 Stream Cipher 2018). To realize that, a new version of ZUC has been formed, which accepts 256-bit keys and differs from the 128-bit version only in key loading mechanism. The initialization vector size is still 128 bit and, therefore, the total number states bits needed to load the key and IV is 384, leaving 112 bits to be loaded with pre-decided constants. There are 16 constants $d_0, d_1, \dots d_{15}$ each 7-bit long. The constants are as followed:

$$d_0 = 0100010_2 = 0\text{x}44\text{D}7_{16}, \quad d_1 = 0101111_2 = 0\text{x}2\text{F}_{16},$$
$$d_2 = 0100100_2 = 0\text{x}24_{16}, \quad d_3 = 0101010_2 = 0\text{x}2\text{A}_{16},$$
$$d_4 = 1101101_2 = 0\text{x}4\text{D}_{16}, \quad d_5 = 1000000_2 = 0\text{x}40_{16},$$
$$d_6 = 1000000_2 = 0\text{x}40_{16}, \quad d_7 = 1000000_2 = 0\text{x}40_{16},$$
$$d_8 = 1000000_2 = 0\text{x}40_{16}, \quad d_9 = 1000000_2 = 0\text{x}40_{16},$$
$$d_{10} = 1000000_2 = 0\text{x}40_{16}, \quad d_{11} = 1000000_2 = 0\text{x}40_{16},$$

$$d_{12} = 1000000_2 = 0x40_{16}, \quad d_{13} = 1010010 = 0x25_{16},$$
$$d_{14} = 0010000_2 = 0x10_{16}, \quad d_{15} = 0110000_2 = 0x30_{16}.$$

The key loading procedure for the 256-bit version is as follows:

$$s_0 = K_0 \parallel d_0 \parallel K_{21} \parallel K_{16}, s_1 = K_1 \parallel d_1 \parallel K_{22} \parallel K_{17},$$
$$s_2 = K_2 \parallel d_2 \parallel K_{23} \parallel K_{18}, s_3 = K_3 \parallel d_3 \parallel K_{24} \parallel K_{19},$$
$$s_4 = K_4 \parallel d_4 \parallel K_{25} \parallel K_{20}, s_5 = IV_0 \parallel (d_5|IV_{17}) \parallel K_5 \parallel K_{26},$$
$$s_6 = IV_1 \parallel (d_6|IV_{18}) \parallel K_6 \parallel K_{27}, s_7 = IV_{10} \parallel (d_7|IV_{19}) \parallel K_7 \parallel IV_2,$$
$$s_8 = K_8 \parallel (d_8|IV_{20}) \parallel IV_3 \parallel IV_{11}, s_9 = K_9 \parallel (d_9|IV_{21}) \parallel IV_{12} \parallel IV_4,$$
$$s_{10} = IV_5 \parallel (d_{10}|IV_{22}) \parallel K_{10} \parallel K_{28}, s_{11} = K_{11} \parallel (d_{11}|IV_{23}) \parallel IV_6 \parallel IV_{13},$$
$$s_{12} = K_{12} \parallel (d_{12}|IV_{24}) \parallel IV_7 \parallel IV_{14}, s_{13} = K_{13} \parallel d_{13} \parallel IV_{15} \parallel IV_8,$$
$$s_{14} = K_{14} \parallel (d_{14}|(K_{31})_{4H}) \parallel IV_{16} \parallel IV_9, s_{15} = K_{15} \parallel (d_{15}|(K_{31})_{4L}) \parallel K_{30} \parallel K_{29}.$$

The functioning of the cipher is identical otherwise.

3.6.1 Generation of MAC in ZUC-256

The 256-bit architecture can provide MAC of size 32, 64 or 128 bit as specified by the standard. The procedure is same as in the aforementioned EEA3 protocol. The only difference is that the size of the sliding window is same as the MAC size. Suppose t is the size of the MAC. Then we define $l = \lceil \frac{LENGTH}{32} \rceil + 2 \cdot \frac{t}{32}$. Corresponding to the size of t, Algorithm 3.8 can generate the requisite MAC for a given message M. It is to be noted that the one time mask is added in this version differently.

Algorithm 3.8: MAC of 256-EIA3

---

1 **Input:** $IK \in \{0, 1\}^k, IV \in \{0, 1\}^n, M = (m_0, m_1, \ldots, m_{LENGTH-1}) \in \{0, 1\}^{LENGTH}$;
2 **Output:** MAC;
3 $(x_0, x_1, \ldots, x_{32(l-1)}) \leftarrow S(IK, IV)$;
4        $\triangleright S$ is the output of ZUC when initialized with IK and IV. ;
5 **for** $i = 0$ *to* $LENGTH - 1$ **do**
6 | $W_i \leftarrow x_{i+t}, x_{i+t+1}, \ldots, x_{i+2t-1}$;
7 | **if** $m_i = 1$ **then**
8 | | $MAC \leftarrow MAC \oplus W_i$;
9 | **end**
10 **end**
11 $W_{LENGTH} \leftarrow (x_{LENGTH}, x_{LENGTH+t}, \ldots, x_{LENGTH+2t-1})$;
12 $MAC \leftarrow MAC \oplus W_{LENGTH}$;
13 **return** MAC;

There has already been a work by Ding et al. (2020) on this version of the cipher which claims that a linear approximation attack can recover a key in 2^{236} complexity, which is reported as a weakness of the cipher. However, this does not have any impact on the currently in use 128-bit version.

References

Ding J, Johansson T, Maximov A (2020) Spectral analysis of ZUC-256. In: IACR transactions on symmetric cryptology, vol 2020, no 1, pp 266–288. https://eprint.iacr.org/2019/1352.pdf

Ekdahl P, Johansson T (2002) A new version of the stream cipher SNOW. In: Selected Areas in Cryptography, SAC 2002, pp 515–532. Springer, Berlin

ETSI/SAGE Specification Version: 1.7 Date: 30 th Dec (2011) Specification of the 3GPP Confidentiality and Integrity Algorithms 128-EEA3 & 128-EIA3. Document 1: 128-EEA3 and 128-EIA3 Specification

Specification of the 3GPP Confidentiality and Integrity Algorithms 128-EEA3 and 128-EIA3. Document 4: Design and Evaluation Report. Date: 9th September (2011b). https://www.gsma.com/security/wp-content/uploads/2019/05/EEA3_EIA3_Design_Evaluation_v2_0.doc

Specification of the 3GPP Confidentiality and Integrity Algorithms 128-EEA3 and 128-EIA3. ETSI/SAGE, Document 2: ZUC Specification, Version 1.6, 28th June (2011a). https://www.gsma.com/aboutus/wp-content/uploads/2014/12/eea3eia3zucv16.pdf

Specification of the 3GPP Confidentiality and Integrity Algorithms UEA2 & UIA2. ETSI/SAGE, Document 2: SNOW 3G Specification, 6th September (2006)

The ZUC-256 Stream Cipher (2018). http://www.is.cas.cn/ztzl2016/zouchongzhi/201801/W020180126529970733243.pdf

Wu H, Huang T, Ha Nguyen P, Wang H, Ling S (2012) Differential attacks against stream cipher ZUC. International conference on the theory and application of cryptology and information security (Asiacrypt 2012). Springer, Berlin, pp 262–277

ZUC Stream Cipher. https://asecuritysite.com/encryption/zuc?k=0&iv=0. Last accessed in 2020

Chapter 4
Cryptanalysis on ZUC 1.4

Abstract ZUC has been subject to almost a decade of cryptanalysis at the time of this book. There have been some weaknesses found in the earlier versions of the cipher which has led to the improvement in this cipher. The latest version of ZUC, i.e., ZUC 1.6 has withstood cryptanalysis and has not shown any weaknesses as of now. In this chapter, we go over an analysis of the different part of ZUC cipher and also some of the weaknesses found in the earlier version of the cipher, i.e., ZUC 1.4. We first study a few cryptographic properties of the cipher and then we describe a differential attack on ZUC 1.4. Further, we present a forgery attack on an older integrity protocol of EIA3.

Keywords ZUC · Nonlinearity · Differential uniformity · Differential attack · Forgery attack

4.1 Analysis of ZUC

The most recent version of ZUC has not yet been proven to have any weaknesses in terms of the bit size of its security. However, there are some aspects of the cipher which are not completely random and may be exploited to find an attack on the cipher. Some properties of the different components of the cipher are yet to be conclusively studied as well. In this section, we present the already known non-random behavior of the cipher and point out some questions which can be of interest in further analysis of the cipher. We also understand the reversibility of the cipher and provide corresponding code.

4.1.1 Analysis of the S-Box

The ZUC cipher (Specification of the 3GPP Confidentiality and Integrity Algorithms 128-EEA3 and 128-EIA3 2011a) uses two reversible substitution boxes $S_0 : \{0, 1\}^8 \to \{0, 1\}^8$ and $S_1 : \{0, 1\}^8 \to \{0, 1\}^8$. One of these S-boxes, S_1 is an affine equivalent to the one used in AES. We have already discussed how these two S-boxes have been used to create a 32-bit input 32-bit output S-box called S (see Chap. 3). Here, we revisit the functionality of S-box S. Let $\mathbf{x}$ is a 32-bit input such that $\mathbf{x} = \mathbf{x}_0 \parallel \mathbf{x}_1 \parallel \mathbf{x}_2 \parallel \mathbf{x}_3$, where $\mathbf{x}_i$ are all of size 8 bits, for $i = 0, \ldots, 3$. Then $S(\mathbf{x}) = S_0(\mathbf{x}_0) \parallel S_1(\mathbf{x}_1) \parallel S_0(\mathbf{x}_2) \parallel S_1(\mathbf{x}_3)$, It can be easily verified that the function S is a permutation as well. Suppose $S(\mathbf{x}) = S(\mathbf{y})$ then,

$$S_0(\mathbf{x}_0) \parallel S_1(\mathbf{x}_1) \parallel S_0(\mathbf{x}_2) \parallel S_1(\mathbf{x}_3) = S_0(\mathbf{y}_0) \parallel S_1(\mathbf{y}_1) \parallel S_0(\mathbf{y}_2) \parallel S_1(\mathbf{y}_3)$$

$$\implies \mathbf{x}_0 = \mathbf{y}_0, \mathbf{x}_1 = \mathbf{y}_1, \mathbf{x}_2 = \mathbf{y}_2, \mathbf{x}_3 = \mathbf{y}_3 \text{ [As both } S_0 \text{ and } S_1 \text{ are permutations]}$$

$$\implies \mathbf{x} = \mathbf{y}.$$

Below we list out some of the cryptographic properties   of the S-boxes S_0 and S_1.

$$S_0 : \begin{cases} \text{Nonlinearity} = 96, \\ \text{Differential Uniformity} = 8, \\ \text{Algebraic Degree} = 5, \\ \text{Algebraic Immunity} = 3, \\ \text{Correlation Immunity} = 0. \end{cases} \quad S_1 : \begin{cases} \text{Nonlinearity} = 112, \\ \text{Differential Uniformity} = 4, \\ \text{Algebraic Degree} = 7, \\ \text{Algebraic Immunity} = 4, \\ \text{Correlation Immunity} = 0. \end{cases}$$

The nonlinearity and differential uniformity of these S-boxes are of particular interest, as these secure the cipher against linear cryptanalysis and differential cryptanalysis respectively (see Sect. 1.5 of Chap. 1). Due to this reason, high nonlinearity and low differential uniformity are desired in an S-box.

Now we look at some of the upper and lower bounds of these properties and compare these bounds with the corresponding values of the function $S : \{0, 1\}^{32} \to \{0, 1\}^{32}$ formed using the S-boxes S_0 and S_1.

Property 4.1 *The minimum differential uniformity (see Definition 1.11 of Chap. 1) of a function from $\{0, 1\}^{32}$ to $\{0, 1\}^{32}$ is 2. If a function has differential uniformity 2 then the function is called an Almost Perfect Nonlinear (APN) function.*

Now we calculate the differential uniformity of the S-boxes S. We know that the differential uniformity of S_0 is 8. Hence, there exists $\mathbf{a} \neq \mathbf{0}$ and $\mathbf{b}$ such that $|\mathbf{x} : S_0(\mathbf{x}) \oplus_8 S_0(\mathbf{x} \oplus_8 \mathbf{a}) = \mathbf{b}| = 8$. We now construct two 32-bit values $\mathbf{a}_0 = \mathbf{a} \parallel 0_8 \parallel 0_8 \parallel 0_8$ and $\mathbf{b}_0 = \mathbf{b} \parallel 0_8 \parallel 0_8 \parallel 0_8$. It can be observed that,

$$|\mathbf{x} : S(\mathbf{x}) \oplus_{32} S(\mathbf{x} \oplus_{32} \mathbf{a}_0) = \mathbf{b}_0| = 8 \times 2^8 \times 2^8 \times 2^8 = 2^{27}.$$

Hence, the differential uniformity of S is 2^{27} which is quite higher than the desired value.

Now, we study the nonlinearity of S. Before that, we state the following property.

Property 4.2 *The maximum nonlinearity of an S-box $S : \{0, 1\}^n \to \{0, 1\}^n$ is $2^{n-1} - 2^{\frac{n+1}{2}}$.*

Nonlinearity of the function S is also bound above by the nonlinearity of S_0. If we just look at the component function corresponding to one of the S boxes, the maximum value of Walsh spectrum is going to be the same as that of the 8-variable smaller S-box. As we have already discussed that the Walsh spectrum of an S-box of form $\{0, 1\}^n \rightarrow \{0, 1\}^n$ contains the Walsh spectrum values corresponding to all its component functions $c \cdot S(x)$, where $c \in \{0, 1\}^n \setminus \{0\}$ (see Definition 1.8 of Chap. 1). We choose c to be $c_1 \parallel 0_8 \parallel 0_8 \parallel 0_8$ such that the component of S_0 that has the highest Walsh spectrum value is $c_1 \cdot S_0$. Then the maximum Walsh spectrum value of $c \cdot S$ is same as that of the maximum of the S-box S_0. Hence, the nonlinearity of S is upper bounded by that of S_0, which is 96. As with the differential uniformity, this is far from the optimal value.

Boolean functions formed by the concatenation of smaller boolean functions seldom have optimal cryptographic properties. However, this procedure is still widely used to keep the complexity of the circuit size low. From [9], it can be observed that, in most of the cases, the number of gates required to implement any n-variable Boolean function is $\Theta(\frac{2^n}{n})$. In this case, as the S-box $S : \{0, 1\}^{32} \rightarrow \{0, 1\}^{32}$ is formed by concatenating S-boxes $S_0, S_1 : \{0, 1\}^8 \rightarrow \{0, 1\}^8$, hence, the implementation can simply be done using 4 circuits with 8-bit input 8-bit output. This would be manageable in a practical scenario. On the other hand, forming a circuit for a 32-bit input 32-bit output S-box can require $\Theta(\frac{2^{32}}{32})$ gates which will be very difficult to manage in a real scenario. In fact, the restriction on the number of gates is even stricter than usual in this case. This is because the confidentiality algorithms of mobile telephony are situated in the hardware terminal of the mobile equipment and the number of gates available in the handset for this purpose is often few. An interesting fact on this direction is that the popular cipher AES was not used as the core of any of the standards for third-generation confidentiality algorithms because the number of gates allowed in that generation for implementing confidentiality algorithms were not enough for AES.

4.1.2 Reversibility of ZUC

The current version of ZUC 1.6 is reversible, i.e., given the state of the LFSR and the value of the register R_1 and R_2 at some time instance t, the state of the LFSR and registers R_1, R_2 at any instance $t - i$ can be found, where $1 \leq i \leq t$. The reversibility of ZUC is dependent on the reversibility of each of the layer. We first start with the reversibility of the nonlinear function F.

4.1.2.1 Reversibility of Nonlinear Function F

We start by revisiting the pseudo-code of the nonlinear function F presented in Algorithm 3.1 before discussing about its reversibility. Suppose the value of R_1 and

R_2 at tth clock is R_1^t and R_2^t. To show that F is reversible we need to show that there is a one-to-one correspondence between R_1^t to R_1^{t-1} and R_2^t to R_2^{t-1}. It means, R_1^{t-1} and R_2^{t-1} can uniquely be determined given the value of R_1^t and R_2^t. We describe the algorithm of F in terms of instances at $t-1$ and t to have a clear understanding. At an instance t, the input to the function F are X_0^{t-1}, X_1^{t-1} and X_2^{t-1} (see Algorithm 3.1). Then from the Algorithm 3.1, we have the followings,

1. $W = (X_0^{t-1} \oplus R_1^{t-1}) \boxplus R_2^{t-1}$,
2. $W_1 = R_1^{t-1} \boxplus X_1^{t-1}$,
3. $W_2 = R_2^{t-1} \oplus X_2^{t-1}$,
4. $R_1^t = S(\mathcal{L}_1(W_{1L} \| W_{2H}))$,
5. $R_2^t = S(\mathcal{L}_2(W_{2L} \| W_{1H}))$.

To invert the nonlinear function F first, we need to find $\mathcal{L}_1(W_{1L} \| W_{2H})$ and $\mathcal{L}_2(W_{2L} \| W_{1H})$ from R_1^t and R_2^t respectively. Let $\mathcal{L}_1(W_{1L} \| W_{2H})=V_1$ and $\mathcal{L}_2(W_{2L} \| W_{1H}) = V_2$ which are the inputs to the S-box. These V_1, V_2 can easily be found uniquely from R_1^t and R_2^t as the S-box S is invertible. Let us consider $S(\mathbf{x}) = \mathbf{y}$, where $\mathbf{y} = \mathbf{y}_0 \| \mathbf{y}_1 \| \mathbf{y}_2 \| \mathbf{y}_3$, $\mathbf{x} = \mathbf{x}_0 \| \mathbf{x}_1 \| \mathbf{x}_2 \| \mathbf{x}_3$ and $\mathbf{y}_0 = S_0(\mathbf{x}_0)$, $\mathbf{y}_1 = S_1(\mathbf{x}_1)$, $\mathbf{y}_2 = S_0(\mathbf{x}_2)$ and $\mathbf{y}_3 = S_1(\mathbf{x}_3)$. As S_0 and S_1 both are invertible, so $\mathbf{x}_0$, $\mathbf{x}_1$, $\mathbf{x}_2$ and $\mathbf{x}_3$ can be obtained from $\mathbf{y}_0$, $\mathbf{y}_1$, $\mathbf{y}_2$ and $\mathbf{y}_3$ respectively. The C-code snippet for creating the inverses of S-boxes S_0, S_1 are provided in Code 4.1.

```
1  //S0i is the inverse of S0 and S1i is the inverse of S1
2  int i;
3  int *S0i=(int *)malloc(sizeof(int)*256);
4  int *S1i=(int *)malloc(sizeof(int)*256);
5  for(i=0;i<256;i++)
6  {
7      S0i[S0[i]]=i;
8      S1i[S1[i]]=i;
9  }
```

Code 4.1 Inverse of S-boxes S_0 and S_1

Now the next step is given the value of V_1 and V_2 we need to find the values of $W_{1L} \| W_{2H}$ and $W_{2L} \| W_{1H}$. Once we have these values, as we have the values of X_0^{t-1} and X_1^{t-1}, we can find out the values of R_1^{t-1} and R_2^{t-1} uniquely. To find the values of $W_{1L} \| W_{2H}$ and $W_{2L} \| W_{1H}$ from V_1 and V_2, we need to look into the invertibility of linear the transformations $\mathcal{L}_1$ and $\mathcal{L}_2$.

Reversibility of the Linear Transformations $\mathcal{L}_1$ and $\mathcal{L}_2$

We first start with the linear transformation $\mathcal{L}_1$. We recall the definition of $\mathcal{L}_1$, which is $\mathcal{L}_1(X) = X \oplus (X \lll_{32} 2) \oplus (X \lll_{32} 10) \oplus (X \lll_{32} 18) \oplus (X \lll_{32} 24)$.

The linear transformation $\mathcal{L}_1$ takes a 32-bit input and gives a 32-bit output. Let the input be $\mathbf{a} = a_{31}a_{30}a_{29} \cdots a_1a_0$ and the corresponding output be $\mathcal{L}_1(\mathbf{a}) = \mathbf{b} = b_{31}b_{30}b_{29} \cdots b_1b_0$. As $\mathcal{L}_1$ is a linear transformation, so the output bits can be expressed as linear combinations of input bits. The linear relations between input and output bits will be as follows:

$$b_0 = a_0 \oplus a_{30} \oplus a_{22} \oplus a_{14} \oplus a_8$$
$$b_1 = a_1 \oplus a_{31} \oplus a_{23} \oplus a_{15} \oplus a_9$$
$$\vdots$$
$$b_{31} = a_{31} \oplus a_{29} \oplus a_{21} \oplus a_{13} \oplus a_7.$$

(4.1)

To find the inverse of $\mathcal{L}_1$, one needs to find the solution of the system of Eq. (4.1) by considering $b_i : 0 \le i \le 31$ as known and $a_i : 0 \le i \le 31$ as unknowns. The problem therefore reduces to solving this system of linear equations over $GF(2)$.

First, we need to check that whether the system of Eq. 4.1 has a unique solution or not. Since there are 32 equations and 32 unknowns, if the rank of the corresponding coefficient matrix is 32, then there is a unique solution for **a**. We use L_1 to denote this matrix. Similarly, one can construct a system of linear equations over $GF(2)$ for the linear transformation $\mathcal{L}_2$. Let the corresponding coefficient matrix be L_2. The matrices L_1 and L_2 are described in Eqs. 4.2 and 4.3 respectively.

$$L_1 = \begin{bmatrix}
1&0&0&0&0&0&0&0&1&0&0&0&0&0&1&0&0&0&0&0&0&0&1&0&0&0&0&0&0&0&1&0\\
0&1&0&0&0&0&0&0&0&1&0&0&0&0&0&1&0&0&0&0&0&0&0&1&0&0&0&0&0&0&0&1\\
1&0&1&0&0&0&0&0&0&0&1&0&0&0&0&0&1&0&0&0&0&0&0&0&1&0&0&0&0&0&0&0\\
0&1&0&1&0&0&0&0&0&0&0&1&0&0&0&0&0&1&0&0&0&0&0&0&0&1&0&0&0&0&0&0\\
0&0&1&0&1&0&0&0&0&0&0&0&1&0&0&0&0&0&1&0&0&0&0&0&0&0&1&0&0&0&0&0\\
0&0&0&1&0&1&0&0&0&0&0&0&0&1&0&0&0&0&0&1&0&0&0&0&0&0&0&1&0&0&0&0\\
0&0&0&0&1&0&1&0&0&0&0&0&0&0&1&0&0&0&0&0&1&0&0&0&0&0&0&0&1&0&0&0\\
0&0&0&0&0&1&0&1&0&0&0&0&0&0&0&1&0&0&0&0&0&1&0&0&0&0&0&0&0&1&0&0\\
0&0&0&0&0&0&1&0&1&0&0&0&0&0&0&0&1&0&0&0&0&0&1&0&0&0&0&0&0&0&1&0\\
0&0&0&0&0&0&0&1&0&1&0&0&0&0&0&0&0&1&0&0&0&0&0&1&0&0&0&0&0&0&0&1\\
1&0&0&0&0&0&0&0&1&0&1&0&0&0&0&0&0&0&1&0&0&0&0&0&1&0&0&0&0&0&0&0\\
0&1&0&0&0&0&0&0&0&1&0&1&0&0&0&0&0&0&0&1&0&0&0&0&0&1&0&0&0&0&0&0\\
0&0&1&0&0&0&0&0&0&0&1&0&1&0&0&0&0&0&0&0&1&0&0&0&0&0&1&0&0&0&0&0\\
0&0&0&1&0&0&0&0&0&0&0&1&0&1&0&0&0&0&0&0&0&1&0&0&0&0&0&1&0&0&0&0\\
0&0&0&0&1&0&0&0&0&0&0&0&1&0&1&0&0&0&0&0&0&0&1&0&0&0&0&0&1&0&0&0\\
0&0&0&0&0&1&0&0&0&0&0&0&0&1&0&1&0&0&0&0&0&0&0&1&0&0&0&0&0&1&0&0\\
0&0&0&0&0&0&1&0&0&0&0&0&0&0&1&0&1&0&0&0&0&0&0&0&1&0&0&0&0&0&1&0\\
0&0&0&0&0&0&0&1&0&0&0&0&0&0&0&1&0&1&0&0&0&0&0&0&0&1&0&0&0&0&0&1\\
0&0&0&0&0&0&0&1&0&0&0&0&0&0&1&0&1&0&0&0&0&0&0&0&1&0&0&0&0&0&1\\
1&0&0&0&0&0&0&1&0&0&0&0&0&0&1&0&1&0&0&0&0&0&0&1&0&0&0&0&0&1&0&0\\
0&1&0&0&0&0&0&1&0&0&0&0&0&0&1&0&1&0&0&0&0&0&0&1&0&0&0&0&1&0&0&0\\
0&0&1&0&0&0&0&0&1&0&0&0&0&0&0&1&0&1&0&0&0&0&0&0&1&0&0&0&0&1&0&0\\
0&0&0&1&0&0&0&0&0&1&0&0&0&0&0&0&1&0&1&0&0&0&0&0&0&1&0&0&0&0&1&0\\
0&0&0&0&1&0&0&0&0&0&1&0&0&0&0&0&0&1&0&1&0&0&0&0&0&0&1&0&0&0&0&1\\
1&0&0&0&0&1&0&0&0&0&0&1&0&0&0&0&0&0&1&0&1&0&0&0&0&0&0&1&0&0&0&0\\
0&1&0&0&0&0&1&0&0&0&0&0&1&0&0&0&0&0&0&1&0&1&0&0&0&0&0&0&1&0&0&0\\
0&0&1&0&0&0&0&1&0&0&0&0&0&1&0&0&0&0&0&0&1&0&1&0&0&0&0&0&0&1&0&0\\
0&0&0&1&0&0&0&0&1&0&0&0&0&0&1&0&0&0&0&0&0&1&0&1&0&0&0&0&0&0&1&0\\
0&0&0&0&1&0&0&0&0&1&0&0&0&0&0&1&0&0&0&0&0&0&1&0&1&0&0&0&0&0&0&1\\
0&0&0&0&0&1&0&0&0&0&1&0&0&0&0&0&1&0&0&0&0&0&0&1&0&1&0&0&0&0&0&0\\
0&0&0&0&0&0&1&0&0&0&0&1&0&0&0&0&0&1&0&0&0&0&0&0&1&0&1&0&0&0&0&0\\
0&0&0&0&0&0&0&1&0&0&0&0&1&0&0&0&0&0&1&0&0&0&0&0&0&1&0&0&0&0&1&0&1
\end{bmatrix}$$

(4.2)

$$
L_2 =
\begin{bmatrix}
1 0 1 0 0 0 0 0 0 0 1 0 0 0 0 0 0 0 1 0 0 0 0 0 1 0 0 0 0 0 0 0 \\
0 1 0 1 0 0 0 0 0 0 0 1 0 0 0 0 0 0 0 1 0 0 0 0 0 1 0 0 0 0 0 0 \\
0 0 1 0 1 0 0 0 0 0 0 0 1 0 0 0 0 0 0 0 1 0 0 0 0 0 1 0 0 0 0 0 \\
0 0 0 1 0 1 0 0 0 0 0 0 0 1 0 0 0 0 0 0 0 1 0 0 0 0 0 1 0 0 0 0 \\
0 0 0 0 1 0 1 0 0 0 0 0 0 0 1 0 0 0 0 0 0 0 1 0 0 0 0 0 1 0 0 0 \\
0 0 0 0 0 1 0 1 0 0 0 0 0 0 0 1 0 0 0 0 0 0 0 1 0 0 0 0 0 1 0 0 \\
0 0 0 0 0 0 1 0 1 0 0 0 0 0 0 0 1 0 0 0 0 0 0 0 1 0 0 0 0 0 1 0 \\
0 0 0 0 0 0 0 1 0 1 0 0 0 0 0 0 0 1 0 0 0 0 0 0 0 1 0 0 0 0 0 1 \\
1 0 0 0 0 0 1 0 1 0 0 0 0 0 0 0 1 0 0 0 0 0 0 0 1 0 0 0 0 0 0 0 \\
0 1 0 0 0 0 0 1 0 1 0 0 0 0 0 0 0 1 0 0 0 0 0 0 0 1 0 0 0 0 0 0 \\
0 0 1 0 0 0 0 0 1 0 1 0 0 0 0 0 0 0 1 0 0 0 0 0 0 0 1 0 0 0 0 0 \\
0 0 0 1 0 0 0 0 0 1 0 1 0 0 0 0 0 0 0 1 0 0 0 0 0 0 0 1 0 0 0 0 \\
0 0 0 0 1 0 0 0 0 0 1 0 1 0 0 0 0 0 0 0 1 0 0 0 0 0 0 0 1 0 0 0 \\
0 0 0 0 0 1 0 0 0 0 0 1 0 1 0 0 0 0 0 0 0 1 0 0 0 0 0 0 0 1 0 0 \\
1 0 0 0 0 0 1 0 0 0 0 0 1 0 1 0 0 0 0 0 0 0 1 0 0 0 0 0 0 0 0 0 \\
0 1 0 0 0 0 0 1 0 0 0 0 0 1 0 1 0 0 0 0 0 0 0 1 0 0 0 0 0 0 0 0 \\
0 0 1 0 0 0 0 0 1 0 0 0 0 0 1 0 1 0 0 0 0 0 0 0 1 0 0 0 0 0 0 0 \\
0 0 0 1 0 0 0 0 0 1 0 0 0 0 0 1 0 1 0 0 0 0 0 0 0 1 0 0 0 0 0 0 \\
0 0 0 0 1 0 0 0 0 0 1 0 0 0 0 0 1 0 1 0 0 0 0 0 0 0 1 0 0 0 0 0 \\
0 0 0 0 0 1 0 0 0 0 0 1 0 0 0 0 0 1 0 1 0 0 0 0 0 0 0 1 0 0 0 0 \\
0 0 0 0 0 0 1 0 0 0 0 0 1 0 0 0 0 0 1 0 1 0 0 0 0 0 0 0 1 0 0 0 \\
0 0 0 0 0 0 0 1 0 0 0 0 0 1 0 0 0 0 0 1 0 1 0 0 0 0 0 0 0 1 0 0 \\
1 0 0 0 0 0 0 0 1 0 0 0 0 0 1 0 0 0 0 0 1 0 1 0 0 0 0 0 0 0 0 0 \\
0 1 0 0 0 0 0 0 0 1 0 0 0 0 0 1 0 0 0 0 0 1 0 1 0 0 0 0 0 0 0 0 \\
0 0 1 0 0 0 0 0 0 0 1 0 0 0 0 0 1 0 0 0 0 0 1 0 1 0 0 0 0 0 0 0 \\
0 0 0 1 0 0 0 0 0 0 0 1 0 0 0 0 0 1 0 0 0 0 0 1 0 1 0 0 0 0 0 0 \\
0 0 0 0 1 0 0 0 0 0 0 0 1 0 0 0 0 0 1 0 0 0 0 0 1 0 1 0 0 0 0 0 \\
0 0 0 0 0 1 0 0 0 0 0 0 0 1 0 0 0 0 0 1 0 0 0 0 0 1 0 1 0 0 0 0 \\
0 0 0 0 0 0 1 0 0 0 0 0 0 0 1 0 0 0 0 0 1 0 0 0 0 0 1 0 1 0 0 0 \\
0 0 0 0 0 0 0 1 0 0 0 0 0 0 0 1 0 0 0 0 0 1 0 0 0 0 0 1 0 1 0 0 \\
1 0 0 0 0 0 0 0 1 0 0 0 0 0 0 0 1 0 0 0 0 0 1 0 0 0 0 0 1 0 1 0 \\
0 1 0 0 0 0 0 0 0 1 0 0 0 0 0 0 0 1 0 0 0 0 0 1 0 0 0 0 0 1 0 1
\end{bmatrix}
\tag{4.3}
$$

The rank of both of these matrices are 32 which ensures a unique solution given any value of **b**. Hence, one can uniquely determine $\mathbf{a}_1$, $\mathbf{a}_2$ from $\mathcal{L}_1(\mathbf{a}_1)$ and $\mathbf{a}_\epsilon$ respectively. These solution can be obtained by using Gaussian elimination method, which takes $O(n^3)$ time, where $n = 32$. Since there are two systems of linear equations corresponding to $\mathcal{L}_1$ and $\mathcal{L}_2$, so finding the input to $\mathcal{L}_1$ and $\mathcal{L}_2$ will take approximately $2 \times 32^3 = 2^{16}$ clock cycles. The time complexity of this procedure is thus very high compared to the forward implementation of the transformations. Therefore, we attempt to generalize the solution in terms of $b_{31}, b_{30}, \ldots b_0$. We want to find the solution to the system of equation $L\mathbf{a} = \mathbf{b}$. Since the equations are linear, the problem can be expressed as

$$
b_i = \oplus_{j=0}^{n-1} c_{ij} a_j, \text{ where } c_{ij} \in \{0, 1\}, i = 0, \ldots, n-1. \tag{4.4}
$$

We aim to find values of u_{ij} such that $a_i = \oplus_{j=0}^{n-1} u_{ij} b_j$, where $u_{ij} \in 0, 1, i = 0, \ldots, n-1$. We use the Gaussian elimination method to calculate the values of u_{ij} so that given the values of b_i, we can find out a_i directly without having to implement Gaussian elimination every time. These coefficients $u_{ij}, i, j = 0, 1, \ldots, n-1$ forms the inverse matrix (say L_1^{-1}) and thus $L_1^{-1} b = a$. The C-code presented in Code 4.2 achieves this objective. The implementation is quite simple and self-explanatory.

```
1   for(i=0;i<N;i++)
2       *(res+i)=(int *)calloc(sizeof(int),N);
3   /* res[N][N] stores the inverse function
4       mat[N][N] represents the linear transformation
5       N=32 */
6   for(i=0;i<N;i++)
7       res[i][i]=1;
8
9   for(i=0;i<N;i++)
10  {
11      if(mat[i][i]!=1)
12      {
13      /* if at ith step, mat[i][i] is not 1,
14          then we add a row with index higher than i
15          with the ith row to make mat[i][i] 1   */
16          printf("not 1 i=%d \n",i);
17          j=i+1;ch=0;
18          while(j<N && ch!=1)
19          {
20              if(mat[j][i]==1)
21              {
22                  for(k=0;k<N;k++)
23                  {
24                      res[i][k]=res[i][k]^res[j][k];
25                      mat[i][k]=mat[i][k]^mat[j][k];
26                  }
27                  ch=1;
28              }
29              else
30                  j++;
31          }
32      }
33      j=0;
34      while(j<N)
35      {
36          /* all the entries of the ith column are made to 0
37              except mat[i][i] */
38          if(j!=i && mat[j][i]==1)
39          {
40              printf("i=%d j=%d \n",i,j);
41              for(k=0;k<N;k++)
42              {
43                  mat[j][k]=mat[j][k]^mat[i][k];
44                  res[j][k]=res[j][k]^res[i][k];
45              }
46          }
47      j++;
48      }
49  }
```

Code 4.2 Inverse linear transformation

By using the Code 4.2, we find the inverse of matrices L_1 and L_2, which are described in Eqs. (4.5) and (4.6) respectively.

$$L_1^{-1} = \begin{bmatrix}
1&0&1&0&0&0&0&0&1&0&1&0&0&0&1&0&1&0&1&0&1&0&0&0&1&0&0&0&1&0&1&0\\
0&1&0&1&0&0&0&0&0&1&0&1&0&0&0&1&0&1&0&1&0&1&0&0&0&1&0&0&0&1&0&1\\
1&0&1&0&1&0&0&0&0&0&1&0&1&0&0&0&1&0&1&0&1&0&1&0&0&0&1&0&0&0&1&0\\
0&1&0&1&0&1&0&0&0&0&0&1&0&1&0&0&0&1&0&1&0&1&0&1&0&0&0&1&0&0&0&1\\
1&0&1&0&1&0&1&0&0&0&0&0&1&0&1&0&0&0&1&0&1&0&1&0&1&0&0&0&1&0&0&0\\
0&1&0&1&0&1&0&1&0&0&0&0&0&1&0&1&0&0&0&1&0&1&0&1&0&1&0&0&0&1&0&0\\
0&0&1&0&1&0&1&0&1&0&0&0&0&0&1&0&1&0&0&0&1&0&1&0&1&0&1&0&0&0&1&0\\
0&0&0&1&0&1&0&1&0&1&0&0&0&0&0&1&0&1&0&0&0&1&0&1&0&1&0&1&0&0&0&1\\
1&0&0&0&1&0&1&0&1&0&0&0&0&0&1&0&1&0&0&0&1&0&1&0&1&0&1&0&1&0&0&0\\
0&1&0&0&0&1&0&1&0&1&0&0&0&0&0&1&0&1&0&0&0&1&0&1&0&1&0&1&0&1&0&0\\
0&0&1&0&0&0&1&0&1&0&1&0&0&0&0&0&1&0&1&0&0&0&1&0&1&0&1&0&1&0&1&0\\
0&0&0&1&0&0&0&1&0&1&0&1&0&0&0&0&0&1&0&1&0&0&0&1&0&1&0&1&0&1&0&1\\
1&0&0&0&1&0&0&0&1&0&1&0&1&0&0&0&0&0&1&0&1&0&0&0&1&0&1&0&1&0&1&0\\
0&1&0&0&0&1&0&0&0&1&0&1&0&1&0&1&0&0&0&0&1&0&1&0&0&0&1&0&1&0&1&0\\
1&0&1&0&0&0&1&0&0&0&1&0&1&0&1&0&0&0&0&0&1&0&1&0&0&0&1&0&1&0&1&0\\
0&1&0&1&0&0&0&1&0&0&0&1&0&1&0&1&0&0&0&0&0&1&0&1&0&0&0&1&0&1&0&1\\
1&0&1&0&0&0&1&0&0&0&1&0&1&0&1&0&1&0&0&0&0&0&1&0&1&0&0&0&1&0&1&0\\
0&1&0&1&0&0&0&1&0&0&0&1&0&1&0&1&0&1&0&0&0&0&0&1&0&1&0&0&0&1&0&1\\
1&0&1&0&1&0&0&0&1&0&0&0&1&0&1&0&1&0&1&0&0&0&0&0&1&0&1&0&0&0&1&0\\
0&1&0&1&0&1&0&0&0&1&0&0&0&1&0&1&0&1&0&1&0&0&0&0&0&1&0&1&0&0&0&1\\
0&0&1&0&1&0&1&0&0&0&1&0&0&0&1&0&1&0&1&0&1&0&0&0&0&0&1&0&1&0&0&0\\
0&0&0&1&0&1&0&1&0&0&0&1&0&0&0&1&0&1&0&1&0&1&0&0&0&0&0&1&0&1&0&0\\
0&0&1&0&1&0&1&0&1&0&0&0&1&0&0&0&1&0&1&0&1&0&1&0&0&0&0&0&1&0&1&0\\
0&0&0&1&0&1&0&1&0&1&0&0&0&1&0&0&0&1&0&1&0&1&0&1&0&0&0&0&0&1&0&1\\
1&0&0&0&1&0&1&0&1&0&0&0&1&0&0&0&1&0&1&0&1&0&1&0&0&0&0&0&0&0&1&0\\
0&1&0&0&0&1&0&1&0&1&0&0&0&1&0&0&0&1&0&1&0&1&0&1&0&0&0&0&0&0&0&1\\
1&0&1&0&0&0&1&0&1&0&1&0&0&0&1&0&0&0&1&0&1&0&1&0&1&0&0&0&0&0&0&0\\
0&1&0&1&0&0&0&1&0&1&0&1&0&0&0&1&0&0&0&1&0&1&0&1&0&1&0&0&0&0&0&0\\
0&0&1&0&1&0&0&0&1&0&1&0&1&0&0&0&1&0&0&0&1&0&1&0&1&0&1&0&0&0&0&0\\
0&0&0&1&0&1&0&0&0&1&0&1&0&1&0&0&0&1&0&0&0&1&0&1&0&1&0&1&0&0&0&0\\
1&0&0&0&0&0&1&0&1&0&0&0&1&0&1&0&1&0&0&0&1&0&0&0&1&0&1&0&1&0&0&0\\
0&1&0&0&0&0&0&1&0&1&0&0&0&1&0&1&0&1&0&0&0&1&0&0&0&1&0&1&0&1&0&1
\end{bmatrix} \tag{4.5}$$

$$L_2^{-1} = \begin{bmatrix}
1&0&1&0&1&0&0&0&1&0&0&0&1&0&1&0&1&0&1&0&0&0&1&0&1&0&0&0&0&0&1&0\\
0&1&0&1&0&1&0&0&0&1&0&0&0&1&0&1&0&1&0&1&0&0&0&1&0&1&0&0&0&0&0&1\\
1&0&1&0&1&0&1&0&0&0&1&0&0&0&1&0&1&0&1&0&1&0&0&0&1&0&1&0&0&0&0&0\\
0&1&0&1&0&1&0&1&0&0&0&1&0&0&0&1&0&1&0&1&0&1&0&0&0&1&0&1&0&0&0&0\\
0&0&1&0&1&0&1&0&1&0&0&0&1&0&0&0&1&0&1&0&1&0&1&0&0&0&1&0&1&0&0&0\\
0&0&0&1&0&1&0&1&0&1&0&0&0&1&0&1&0&1&0&1&0&1&0&1&0&0&0&1&0&1&0&0\\
0&0&0&0&1&0&1&0&1&0&0&0&1&0&0&0&1&0&1&0&1&0&1&0&0&0&1&0&1&0&1&0\\
0&0&0&0&0&1&0&1&0&1&0&0&0&1&0&0&0&1&0&1&0&1&0&1&0&0&0&1&0&1&0&1\\
1&0&0&0&0&0&1&0&1&0&1&0&0&0&1&0&0&0&1&0&1&0&1&0&1&0&0&0&1&0&1&0\\
0&1&0&0&0&0&0&1&0&1&0&1&0&0&0&1&0&0&0&1&0&1&0&1&0&1&0&0&0&1&0&1\\
1&0&1&0&0&0&0&0&1&0&1&0&1&0&0&0&1&0&0&0&1&0&1&0&1&0&1&0&0&0&1&0\\
0&1&0&1&0&0&0&0&0&1&0&1&0&1&0&0&0&1&0&0&0&1&0&1&0&1&0&1&0&0&0&0\\
0&0&1&0&1&0&0&0&0&0&1&0&1&0&1&0&0&0&1&0&0&0&1&0&1&0&1&0&1&0&1&0\\
0&0&0&1&0&1&0&0&0&0&0&1&0&1&0&1&0&0&0&1&0&0&0&1&0&1&0&1&0&1&0&1\\
1&0&0&0&1&0&1&0&0&0&0&0&1&0&1&0&1&0&0&0&1&0&0&0&1&0&1&0&1&0&1&0\\
0&1&0&0&0&1&0&1&0&0&0&0&1&0&1&0&1&0&0&0&1&0&0&0&1&0&1&0&1&0&1&1\\
1&0&1&0&0&0&1&0&1&0&0&0&0&0&1&0&1&0&1&0&0&0&1&0&0&0&1&0&1&0&1&0\\
0&1&0&1&0&0&0&1&0&1&0&0&0&0&0&1&0&1&0&1&0&1&0&0&0&1&0&0&0&1&0&1\\
1&0&1&0&1&0&0&0&1&0&1&0&0&0&0&0&1&0&1&0&1&0&1&0&0&0&1&0&0&0&1&0\\
0&1&0&1&0&1&0&0&0&1&0&1&0&0&0&0&0&1&0&1&0&1&0&1&0&0&0&1&0&0&0&1\\
1&0&1&0&1&0&1&0&0&0&1&0&1&0&0&0&0&0&1&0&1&0&1&0&1&0&0&0&1&0&0&0\\
0&1&0&1&0&1&0&1&0&0&0&1&0&1&0&0&0&0&0&1&0&1&0&1&0&1&0&0&0&1&0&0\\
0&0&1&0&1&0&1&0&1&0&0&0&1&0&0&0&0&0&0&0&1&0&1&0&1&0&1&0&0&0&1&0\\
0&0&0&1&0&1&0&1&0&1&0&0&0&1&0&0&0&1&0&0&0&0&1&0&1&0&1&0&1&0&0&1\\
1&0&0&0&1&0&1&0&1&0&0&0&1&0&0&0&0&0&1&0&1&0&1&0&1&0&0&0&0&0&0&0\\
0&1&0&0&0&1&0&1&0&1&0&1&0&0&0&1&0&1&0&0&0&0&0&1&0&1&0&1&0&1&0&0\\
0&0&1&0&0&0&1&0&1&0&1&0&0&0&1&0&1&0&1&0&0&0&0&0&1&0&1&0&1&0&1&0\\
0&0&0&1&0&0&0&1&0&1&0&1&0&0&0&1&0&1&0&1&0&0&0&0&0&1&0&1&0&1&0&1\\
1&0&0&0&1&0&0&0&1&0&1&0&1&0&0&0&1&0&1&0&1&0&0&0&0&0&1&0&1&0&1&0\\
0&1&0&0&0&1&0&0&0&1&0&1&0&1&0&0&0&1&0&1&0&1&0&0&0&0&0&1&0&1&0&1\\
1&0&1&0&0&0&1&0&0&0&1&0&1&0&1&0&0&0&1&0&1&0&1&0&0&0&0&0&1&0&1&0\\
0&1&0&1&0&0&0&1&0&0&0&1&0&1&0&1&0&0&0&1&0&1&0&1&0&0&0&0&0&1&0&1
\end{bmatrix} \tag{4.6}$$

These matrices L_1^{-1} and L_2^{-1} will generate two different linear transformations $\mathcal{L}_1^{-1}$ and $\mathcal{L}_2^{-1}$ respectively. The algebraic normal from these linear transformations $\mathcal{L}_1^{-1}$ and $\mathcal{L}_2^{-1}$ are described in Eqs. (4.7), (4.8) respectively.

$$\mathcal{L}_1^{-1}(X) = X \oplus (X \lll_{32} 2) \oplus (X \lll_{32} 4) \oplus (X \lll_{32} 8) \oplus (X \lll_{32} 12)$$
$$\oplus (X \lll_{32} 14) \oplus (X \lll_{32} 16) \oplus (X \lll_{32} 18) \oplus (X \lll_{32} 22)$$
$$\oplus (X \lll_{32} 24) \oplus (X \lll_{32} 30), \tag{4.7}$$
$$\mathcal{L}_2^{-1}(X) = X \oplus (X \lll_{32} 2) \oplus (X \lll_{32} 8) \oplus (X \lll_{32} 10) \oplus (X \lll_{32} 14)$$
$$\oplus (X \lll_{32} 16) \oplus (X \lll_{32} 18) \oplus (X \lll_{32} 20) \oplus (X \lll_{32} 24)$$
$$\oplus (X \lll_{32} 28) \oplus (X \lll_{32} 30) \oplus (X \lll_{32} 30). \tag{4.8}$$

From these two inverse transformations, we can find $W_{1L} \parallel W_{2H}$ and $W_{2L} \parallel W_{1H}$, thus the values W_1 and W_2 from V_1 and V_2. Now we only need the values of X_1^{t-1} and X_2^{t-1} to find R_1^{t-1} and R_2^{t-1}. It can be observed that due of the shifting procedure of the LFSR

- $X_1^{t-1} = s_{11L}^{t-1} \parallel s_{9H}^{t-1} = s_{10L}^{t} \parallel s_{8H}^{t}$,
- $X_2^{t-1} = s_{7L}^{t-1} \parallel s_{5H}^{t-1} = s_{6L}^{t} \parallel s_{4H}^{t}$.

Hence, just by shifting the state bits of LFSR, we can find X_1^{t-1} and X_2^{t-1}. Once we have the values of X_1^{t-1} and X_2^{t-1}, we can obtain R_1^{t-1} and R_2^{t-1}.

Here, we provide the compact pseudo-code of the inverse of nonlinear function F in the Algorithm 4.1.

Algorithm 4.1: Reversing the registers of F

1 **Input:** $R_1^t, R_2^t, s_0^t, s_1^t, \ldots, s_{15}^t$;
2 **Output:** R_1^{t-1}, R_2^{t-1};
3 $D_1 \leftarrow S^{-1}(R_1^t)$;
4 $D_2 \leftarrow S^{-1}(R_2^t)$;
5 $D_1 \leftarrow \mathcal{L}_1^{-1}(D_1)$;
6 $D_2 \leftarrow \mathcal{L}_2^{-1}(D_2)$;
7 $W_1 \leftarrow (D_1 \gg 16) + (D_2 \ll 16)$;
8 $W_2 \leftarrow (D_1 \ll 16) + (D_2 \ll 16)$;
9 $X_1^{t-1} \leftarrow (s_{10}^t \ll 16) + (s_8^t \gg 16)$;
10 $X_2^{t-1} \leftarrow (s_6^t \ll 16) + (s_4^t \gg 16)$;
11 $R_1^{t-1} \leftarrow W_1 - X_1^{t-1}$;
12 **if** $R_1^{t-1} \leq 0$ **then**
13 $\quad \mid \quad R_1^{t-1} = R_1^{t-1} + 0\text{x7FFFFFFF}$;
14 **end**
15 $R_2^{t-1} \leftarrow W_2 \oplus X_2^{t-1}$;
16 $res \leftarrow \{R_1^{t-1}, R_2^{t-1}\}$;
17 **return** res ;

The C-code for this reversing process is described in Code 4.3.

```
1  u32 R11,R21;
2  #define ROT(a, k) (((a) << k) | ((a) >> (32 - k)))
3  #define merge32(a, b, c, d) (((u32)(a) << 24) |
4  ((u32)(b) << 16) | ((u32)(c) << 8) | ((u32)(d)))
5  int S0i[256]=
6  {0x6,0x6d,0xc5,0x1e,0x8,0xe5,0x4d,0x90,
7  0x1c,0xc,0x84,0x94,0xe7,0x58,0xc0,0xdf,
8  0x9e,0xb2,0xba,0x86,0x4b,0xd9,0x61,0x63,
9  0xa9,0xfa,0xf2,0x11,0x5f,0x1b,0x33,0x67,
10 0x3d,0x4c,0x85,0xbf,0x66,0xe4,0xa1,0xf1,
11 0x87,0x2d,0xc4,0x95,0x49,0x19,0x6c,0x7e,
12 0xe8,0x53,0x13,0x7,0xfe,0x98,0xd2,0x82,
13 0x3f,0x3b,0x7b,0x70,0x8a,0xda,0x0,0xe6,
14 0xdc,0x99,0xb8,0x35,0xc9,0xf8,0x73,0x3,
15 0x2b,0x5b,0x60,0x71,0x9d,0x20,0x21,0x54,
16 0xd4,0x5a,0x97,0x1d,0xa,0x4e,0x8f,0x46,
17 0x5e,0xb7,0x56,0x2,0xb5,0xaf,0x52,0x5c,
18 0xff,0x9b,0xd7,0x3c,0xb4,0xef,0xb3,0xc7,
19 0xd5,0x36,0x16,0xe3,0xcb,0xe,0x2e,0x7d,
20 0xea,0xd8,0x1,0x34,0xbc,0xb9,0x40,0xe2,
21 0xfd,0x9a,0xf9,0x10,0x88,0x41,0x92,0x55,
22 0x7c,0xf4,0x59,0xe1,0x22,0x2a,0xc1,0x79,
23 0xa3,0x8b,0xa4,0x2c,0x68,0xf0,0xe0,0x78,
24 0x1f,0x27,0x65,0xcd,0xaa,0xa2,0x8e,0x96,
25 0xb,0x23,0x77,0x4f,0xbd,0x15,0xd6,0xce,
26 0xf6,0xec,0xca,0xa6,0x57,0x17,0x9c,0x43,
27 0x64,0xee,0xbe,0xc2,0x2f,0x6f,0x6b,0x14,
28 0xa5,0x80,0x42,0xf5,0x81,0x38,0x29,0xeb,
29 0x18,0xd,0x5d,0x4a,0xa0,0x39,0xc3,0x91,
30 0xa8,0x31,0xcc,0x8d,0xdd,0x47,0x37,0x8c,
31 0x7f,0x75,0x4,0xf,0x89,0x30,0x25,0x44,
32 0xb0,0x9,0xd3,0x6e,0x3e,0x62,0xdb,0x7a,
33 0x6a,0x26,0x72,0xf3,0xb1,0x28,0x76,0xfb,
34 0x5,0xac,0xde,0x50,0x24,0xad,0xc8,0xc6,
35 0xed,0xae,0xe9,0x74,0xb6,0x45,0xfc,0x51,
36 0x93,0xcf,0xab,0x48,0xf7,0xbb,0xd0,0x83,
37 0x32,0x12,0xd1,0xa7,0x1a,0x3a,0x9f,0x69};
38
39 int S1i[256]=
40 {0x17,0xa0,0xbb,0xfd,0xee,0x37,0x43,0xda,
41 0x6e,0x6f,0xdb,0x3c,0x13,0x85,0xde,0xb5,
42 0x28,0x42,0xfc,0x16,0x65,0xaa,0x1a,0x66,
43 0xc6,0x76,0x15,0xc8,0x9b,0x8b,0xd3,0xeb,
44 0x41,0xcf,0x38,0x68,0xa4,0xf9,0x21,0x49,
45 0xef,0xc,0x33,0x60,0xc9,0x88,0x83,0xf4,
46 0x6b,0xd5,0xec,0xd9,0xdf,0xd7,0x44,0x91,
47 0xa7,0x2d,0x30,0x4,0x9,0xe5,0x27,0x73,
48 0x1c,0xd4,0x1f,0x2e,0x20,0x26,0x89,0x6,
49 0x3f,0x9e,0xbc,0x7a,0x52,0x90,0x78,0x58,
50 0xac,0xc3,0x4a,0x61,0xd2,0x0,0x32,0x55,
51 0xa3,0xf5,0xd0,0xb,0x63,0x7d,0x94,0xa6,
52 0xe6,0x74,0x3e,0x2,0xf0,0xed,0x39,0x6c,
53 0x22,0x4c,0xd1,0xc5,0xe7,0x35,0x8a,0xb7,
54 0x72,0x3,0x1b,0x6d,0xcc,0x93,0x29,0xf,
55 0xa8,0xbd,0x5e,0xe8,0xe3,0x6a,0xdd,0x50,
56 0xca,0x24,0x98,0x95,0x51,0xf2,0x7,0x4f,
```

```
57  0xe0,0x9f,0xf6,0x2c,0x10,0x5d,0x77,0x7c,
58  0xab,0xb1,0xd6,0x7b,0x12,0xae,0x23,0x8c,
59  0xe2,0xa9,0x59,0xf3,0x54,0x99,0x96,0x8,
60  0xb8,0x64,0xa5,0xc0,0x56,0x92,0x14,0x2b,
61  0x19,0x7f,0xd,0x97,0xfa,0x80,0x82,0xfb,
62  0xf8,0xe1,0x75,0x36,0xb6,0x31,0xa1,0x71,
63  0xad,0x9a,0xdc,0x4b,0x57,0xa2,0xf1,0x3a,
64  0x34,0x46,0x1,0xbe,0xd8,0x11,0x2a,0xb2,
65  0x5,0x45,0xe9,0x84,0xb9,0x9d,0xb3,0x47,
66  0xb0,0x8e,0x53,0xea,0x4e,0x69,0x5c,0xf7,
67  0x62,0x25,0xa,0x7e,0x3b,0x40,0xbf,0x5a,
68  0x9c,0x2f,0xfe,0x18,0xaf,0x79,0xc4,0xcd,
69  0x8d,0x8f,0xc2,0x5f,0xc7,0xb4,0x70,0xc1,
70  0xba,0x81,0xff,0xe4,0x87,0x4d,0x48,0xcb,
71  0x1e,0x1d,0x3d,0x67,0x86,0xe,0x5b,0xce};
72  /* L1 inverse and L2 inverse */
73  u32 L1i(x)
74  {
75      return ROT(x,30)^ROT(x,24)^ROT(x,22)^ROT(x,18)^ROT(x,16)
76              ^ROT(x,14)^ROT(x,12)^ROT(x,8)^ROT(x,4)^ROT(x,2)^x;
77  }
78  u32 L2i(y)
79  {
80      return ROT(y,30)^ROT(y,28)^ROT(y,24)^ROT(y,20)^ROT(y,18)^
81              ROT(y,16)^ROT(y,14)^ROT(y,10)^ROT(y,8)^ROT(y,2)^y;
82  }
83  FReverse(R1,R2)
84  {
85      u32 v1,v2,Wm1,Wm2,X1m,X2m;
86      /* Inverting the S-boxes */
87      v1=merge32(S0i[R1 >> 24], S1i[(R1 >> 16) & 0xFF],
88                  S0i[(R1 >> 8) & 0xFF], S1i[R1 & 0xFF]);
89      v2=merge32(S0i[R2 >> 24], S1i[(R2 >> 16) & 0xFF],
90                  S0i[(R2 >> 8) & 0xFF], S1i[R2 & 0xFF]);
91      /* Inverting the Linear Transformation */
92      Wm1=L1i(v1); Wm2=L2i(v2);
93      /* Calculating W1 and W2 */
94      W1=(Wm2<<16)|(Wm1>>16);
95      W2=(Wm1<<16)|(Wm2>>16);
96      /* Calculating value of X_1 and X_2 in the previous step */
97      X1m=(LFSR_S10<<16)|(LFSR_S8>>15);
98      X2m=(LFSR_S6<<16)|(LFSR_S4>>15)
99      /* Getting the R_1 and R_2 values at the previous step */
100     R11=W1-X1m;
101     if(R11<=0)
102         R11+=0x7FFFFFFF;
103     R12=X2m^W2;
104 }
```

Code 4.3 Inverse of nonlinear function *F*

Now we discuss the inverse of the LFSR used in ZUC stream cipher.

4.1.2.2 Inverse of the LFSR State Update Process

Since the LFSR has two modes, the reversibility procedure slightly varies with these two modes. We explain the method of reversing the LFSR in the initialization mode, and the reversibility of the working mode follows. Suppose we have the state of the LFSR at an instance t, and we want to reverse it by one step. First, we perform shifting process to find the following state words of $(t-1)$th clock from state words of tth clock.

$$s_i^{t-1} = s_{i-1}^t \text{ where } 1 \le i \le 15$$

Now we only need to calculate the value s_0^{t-1}. In the initialization mode, we know that

$$s_{15}^t = 2^{15}s_{15}^{t-1} + 2^{17}s_{13}^{t-1} + 2^{21}s_{10}^{t-1} + 2^{20}s_4^{t-1} + (2^8 + 1)s_0^{t-1} + (W \gg 1),$$

where W is the output from F at $(t-1)$th instance. As we have already shown, we can find R_1^{t-1} and R_2^{t-1} from R_1^t and R_2^t and thus, we can find output from the nonlinear function at $(t-1)$th instance. So we already know the values of all the entities except s_0^{t-1}. First, we perform the following assignments: $v_1 = s_{15}^t$, $v_2 = 2^{15}s_{15}^{t-1} + 2^{17}s_{13}^{t-1} + 2^{21}s_{10}^{t-1} + 2^{20}s_4^{t-1} + (W \gg 1)$ and $u = s_0^{t-1}$. Now provided any v_1 and v_2 if the equation $v_1 = v_2 + (2^8 + 1)u$ has a unique solution for u, then we can recover s_0^{t-1} uniquely. It is easy to see that given values of v_1 and v_2, there can only be one value of u which will satisfy $v_1 = v_2 + (2^8 + 1)u$. Below we show the uniqueness of such u. We know that $(2^8 + 1)$ is an element in the $GF(2^{31} - 1)$. Therefore, it has a unique inverse. Let that inverse be c, hence, we have the following,

$$(2^8 + 1)u = u_1,$$
$$\implies c(2^8 + 1)u = cu_1,$$
$$\implies u = cu_1.$$

The value of c is found to be $0x55aa55a9$. The C-code of the inverse algorithm is presented in Code 4.4.

```
1
2  LFSRinv()
3  {
4      FReverse(R1,R2);
5      // This gives R11 and R12
6
7      u32 v1,v2,u1,u,f,v;
8
9      //Find X0 at (t-1)th round
10     X0= (LFSR_S14 & 0x FFFF0000)+(LFSR_S13 & 0xFFFF);
11     W= R1^X0+R2;
12     W=W>>1;
13
14     /* W is the output of F at (t-1)th round */
15
```

```
16    /* storing value of LFSR_S15 at instance t
17
18    v1=LFSR_S15;
19
20    /* reversing the states */
21    LFSR_S15=LFSR_S14;   LFSR_S14=LFSR_S13;
22    LFSR_S13=LFSR_S12;   LFSR_S12=LFSR_S11;
23    LFSR_S11=LFSR_S10;   LFSR_S10=LFSR_S9;
24    LFSR_S9=LFSR_S8;     LFSR_S8=LFSR_S7;
25    LFSR_S7=LFSR_S6;     LFSR_S6=LFSR_S5;
26    LFSR_S5=LFSR_S4;     LFSR_S4=LFSR_S3;
27    LFSR_S3=LFSR_S2;     LFSR_S2=LFSR_S1;
28    LFSR_S1=LFSR_S0;
29
30  /* finding LFSR_S0 by finding v2 first. */
31
32    f  = MulByPow2(LFSR_S4,20);
33    v  = MulByPow2(LFSR_S10,21);
34    f  = AddM(f, v);
35    v  = MulByPow2(LFSR_S13,17);
36    f  = AddM(f, v);
37    v  = MulByPow2(LFSR_S15,15);
38    v2 = AddM(f, v);
39    v2 = AddM(v2,W);
40    /* Finding (2^8+1)u */
41
42    if(v1>=v2)
43        u1=v1-v2;
44
45    else
46        u1=v1+0x7FFFFFFF-v2;
47
48    if(u1==0)
49        u1=0x7FFFFFFF;
50
51    u=u1*0x55aa55a9;
52
53    LFSR_S0=u;
```

Code 4.4 Inverse of LFSR state update

From the above discussions, it can be observed that each component of the ZUC 1.6 is invertible and thus the cipher is invertible as a whole.

4.2 Differential Attack on ZUC 1.4

The differential attack on ZUC 1.4 was proposed by Wu et al. (2012). The model of the attack was based on the fact that given a key (K) and two different IVs (IV_1, IV_2) the cipher produces identical keystreams when in one instance the state of the cipher is initialized by (K, IV_1) and other instance of the cipher is initialized by (K, IV_2). This attack exploited the structure of ZUC 1.4 in such a way that given (K, IV_1), (K, IV_2) all the internal states of two instances of the cipher became same after a certain number of rounds of the initialization phase, which in turn resulted in identical keystream bits. We first revisit the working procedure of the LFSR in the initialization mode in ZUC 1.4 in the Algorithm 4.2.

Algorithm 4.2: LFSR Initialization Mode in ZUC 1.4

---

1 **Input:** $s_0, s_1, \ldots, s_{15}, u$ ▷ $u = (w \oplus X_3) \gg 1$ where w is the output of F ;
2 $v \leftarrow (2^{15} s_{15} + 2^{17} s_{13} + 2^{21} s_{10} + 2^{20} s_4 + (1 + 2^8) s_0) \mod (2^{31} - 1)$;
3 $s_{16} \leftarrow (v \oplus u)(2^{31} - 1)$;
4 **if** $s_{16} = 0$ **then**
5 | $s_{16} \leftarrow 2^{31} - 1$;
6 **end**
7 **for** $i = 0$ *to* 15 **do**
8 | $s_i \leftarrow s_{i+1}$;
9 **end**

As we already know, during the initialization phase after loading the key and IV into the state, the cipher will run for 32 clockings, without generating any output (see Sect. 3.2 of Chap. 3).

Now we consider two instances of the cipher ZUC 1.4. We initialize one instance by (K, IV_1) and other one by (K, IV_2). If at the end of the 32 initialization rounds the internal states of both the instances of the cipher are same, then they will produce identical keystreams. The complexity of the attack lies with the number of different choice of (IV_1, IV_2), that could be found for a key K for which the states would be same after the initialization phase. There was a weakness found in the structure which was based on the fact that while updating the LFSR, the output of the nonlinear function is XOR'ed with the feedback value generated by the LFSR. One can easily observe that given a value $x \in GF(2^{31} - 1)$, $x \oplus x = 0$ and $x \oplus \bar{x} = 2^{31} - 1$. But according to the convention used in the design of the cipher, both the values are essentially same, as 0 is converted to $2^{31} - 1$. This observation is used to find out IV pairs such that for an unknown key the states become identically same after l clocking ($l \leq 32$) of the cipher. Now we describe the attack method and obtained results by Wu et al. (2012) in detail.

The attack only considered cases where two IVs IV_1 and IV_2 differs at one byte position. That is given two IVs $IV_1 = (iv_0^{(1)}, \ldots, iv_{15}^{(1)})$ and $IV_2 = (iv_0^{(2)}, \ldots, iv_{15}^{(2)})$, all $iv_i^{(1)}$ and $iv_i^{(2)}$ are equal except one index j for which $iv_j^{(i)} \neq iv_j^{(2)}$. We use Δiv_i to denote the differences between IV_1 and IV_2 at ith byte. The cases are considered for each of the values of $0 \leq i \leq 7$ and then only some cases are considered due to complexity of the other cases.

C1: Consider a case $\Delta iv_i \neq 0$ for $7 \leq i \leq 15$. We can see that the values X_1 and X_2 are fed into the function for updating the registers R_1 and R_2 which are updated via the nonlinear function F. If $i \geq 7$, the difference in iv_i is going to be reflected in the nonlinear function after $i - 7$ clockings of the cipher. This is because the least significant 16 bits of s_7 is fed into X_2. Suppose the difference is at iv_i at start, that is in s_i. After $i - 7$ steps, the value of s_i at start is going to be at s_7 and as s_7's value at any state is fed to the nonlinear function via X_2, the difference in the IV is going to be injected in F.

Which would mean after $i - 7$ steps, $R_2 \neq \widetilde{R_2}$. Now due to the nonlinear nature of F, it becomes very difficult to remove that difference from the registers in F. This is the reason that they didn't consider any IVs with these criteria.

C2: Consider the case $\Delta iv_i \neq 0$ for $2 \leq i \leq 6$. In each of these cases, the difference in iv_i is going to affect the updating process of the LFSR more than once. The least significant 16 bits of the state s_2 is fed to X_3 which is used in the updation of the LFSR. Hence, if $i \geq 2$, the difference would be used in updating the LFSR at least twice. Once when the difference reaches at s_2 after $i - 2$ steps and the second one when it reaches at s_0 after i steps. That means conditions will have to be found so that either in both of the cases of updating the difference is not reflected in the new state s_{15}; otherwise, the difference will be fed into the nonlinear function eventually. This raised the complexity of handling the different propagation and was thus ignored.

C3: Next case is $\Delta iv_i \neq 0$ for at least one i, $0 \leq i \leq 1$. This case is considered in the attack proposed by Wu et al. (2012). We explain the related methodology and the results in the Sect. 4.2.1.

4.2.1 Difference in the First Byte of IV

In this section, we describe the differential attack proposed by Wu et al. (2012). In ZUC 1.4, an 128-bit initialization vector is represented as $iv_{15} \parallel iv_{14} \parallel \cdots \parallel iv_0$ where iv_i is inserted into the least significant 8 bits of the LFSR state word s_i. Therefore the idea of injecting a difference only in the first byte seems both logical and intuitive. We consider two IVs IV_1, IV_2 which differ only in the first byte. After the first clocking of the cipher, the state word containing the first byte themselves get flushed out of the LFSR. As s_0 is involved in the feedback function of the LFSR, so the difference may get propagated to the newly formed s_{15} of the LFSR. The attack finds out instances when this does not occur, i.e., the updated state will be exactly same for both the IVs. If such an instance can be found the cipher will generate identical states for IV_1 and IV_2 after one clocking of the cipher. Hence, in the keystream generation phase, the cipher will generate identical keystream bits.

Now we look at the value of s_{16}, where $s_{15}^t = s_{16}^{t-1}$, i.e., s_{16} is the word created that would be inserted into the LFSR word s_{15} at the end of the current round. We observe the relations between the two IVs so that the difference will be eliminated after the first round of key scheduling phase.

For IV_1 :
$$\begin{cases} s_0 = (k_0 \parallel d_0 \parallel iv_0^{(1)}), \\ v = 2^{15}s_{15} + 2^{17}s_{13} + 2^{21}s_{10} + 2^{20}s_4 + (1 + 2^8)s_0 \mod (2^{31} - 1), \\ s_{16} = v \oplus u. \end{cases}$$

For IV_2 :
$$
\begin{cases}
\tilde{s}_0 = (k_0 \parallel d_0 \parallel iv_0^{(2)}), \\
\tilde{v} = 2^{15}\tilde{s}_{15} + 2^{17}\tilde{s}_{13} + 2^{21}\tilde{s}_{10} + 2^{20}\tilde{s}_4 + (1 + 2^8)\tilde{s}_0 \quad \bmod (2^{31} - 1), \\
\tilde{s}_{16} = v \oplus \tilde{u}.
\end{cases}
$$

As (K, IV_1) and (K, IV_2) are used to initialize two instances of the cipher, all the state words s_i, where $1 \leq i \leq 15$ are identical as the $\Delta iv_i = 0$ for $1 \leq i \leq 15$. We rewrite the equation to identify the difference injected in terms of Δiv_0. As $s_i = \tilde{s}_i$ $1 \leq i \leq 15$ are same for both the instances corresponding to IV_1 and IV_2. So $2^{15}s_{15} + 2^{17}s_{13} + 2^{21}s_{10} + 2^{20}s_4 = 2^{15}\tilde{s}_{15} + 2^{17}\tilde{s}_{13} + 2^{21}\tilde{s}_{10} + 2^{20}\tilde{s}_4$, we use $temp$ to denote $2^{15}s_{15} + 2^{17}s_{13} + 2^{21}s_{10} + 2^{20}s_4$.

Then we will have two sets of equations one is corresponding to IV_1 and other one is corresponding to IV_2.

For IV_1 :
$$
\begin{cases}
u = ((w \oplus X_3) \gg 1), \\
v = (temp + (1 + 2^8)(k_0 \parallel d_0 \parallel iv_0^{(1)})) \quad \bmod (2^{31} - 1), \qquad (4.9) \\
s_{16} = v \oplus u.
\end{cases}
$$

For IV_2 :
$$
\begin{cases}
\tilde{u} = ((w \oplus \tilde{X}_3) \gg 1), \\
\tilde{v} = (temp + (1 + 2^8)(k_0 \parallel d_0 \parallel iv_0^{(2)})) \quad \bmod (2^{31} - 1), \qquad (4.10) \\
\tilde{s}_{16} = \tilde{v} \oplus \tilde{u}.
\end{cases}
$$

First, we look at the difference between v and $\tilde{v}$. With out loss of generality, let us assume $iv_0^{(1)}$ is greater than $iv_0^{(2)}$ and $\Delta iv_0 = iv_0^{(1)} - iv_0^{(2)}$. Then the difference can be calculated as in Eq. (4.11).

$$
\begin{aligned}
v - \tilde{v} &= ((temp + (1 + 2^8)(k_0 \parallel d_0 \parallel iv_0^{(1)})) \\
&\quad - (temp + (1 + 2^8)(k_0 \parallel d_0 \parallel iv_0^{(2)}))) \quad \bmod 2^{31} - 1 \\
&= (1 + 2^8)(k_0 \parallel d_0 \parallel iv_0^{(1)}) - (1 + 2^8)(k_0 \parallel d_0 \parallel iv_0^{(2)}) \quad \bmod 2^{31} - 1 \\
&= (k_0 \parallel d_0 \parallel iv_0^{(1)}) - (k_0 \parallel d_0 \parallel iv_0^{(2)}) \\
&\quad + 2^8((k_0 \parallel d_0 \parallel iv_0^{(1)}) - (k_0 \parallel d_0 \parallel iv_0^{(2)})) \quad \bmod 2^{31} - 1 \\
&= (iv_0^{(1)} - iv_0^{(2)}) + 2^8(iv_0^{(1)} - iv_0^{(2)}) \quad \bmod 2^{31} - 1 \\
&= \Delta iv_0 \parallel \Delta iv_0. \qquad\qquad\qquad\qquad\qquad\qquad\qquad\qquad (4.11)
\end{aligned}
$$

This implies that the most significant 16 bits of v and $\tilde{v}$ are same. As v and $\tilde{v}$ are respectively XOR'ed with u and $\tilde{u}$ and X_1 does not depend on the first byte of IV, so $X_1 = \tilde{X}_1$. Therefore, $u = \tilde{u}$ So, we have the following:

$$
s_{16} = v \oplus u
$$
$$
\tilde{s}_{16} = \tilde{v} \oplus u
$$
$$
v - \tilde{v} = \Delta iv_0 \parallel \Delta iv_0
$$

Here, we want to make s_{16} to be equal to $\widetilde{s_{16}}$ for that we need either of the following set of conditions:

$$\left\{ \begin{array}{l} v \oplus u = 1_{31} \\ \widetilde{v} \oplus u = 0_{31} \quad \text{or} \\ v \oplus \widetilde{v} = 1_{31} \end{array} \right. \qquad \left\{ \begin{array}{l} v \oplus u = 0_{31} \\ \widetilde{v} \oplus u = 1_{31} \\ v \oplus \widetilde{v} = 1_{31} \end{array} \right.$$

Finally, we will need $u = v$ or $u = \widetilde{v}$. It is important to know that the most significant 15 bits of v and $\widetilde{v}$ are the complement of each other, while the difference in the values of v and $\widetilde{v}$ is injected by only addition of $\Delta iv_0 \parallel \Delta iv_0$ in the least significant 16 bits. We write a C-code to observe what are the possible values of v and $\widetilde{v}$ for which this could occur. The code is described in Code 4.5.

```
1  int main()
2  {
3      /*  for all 31 bit numbers, find the scenario that the
4          difference between the number and its compliment
5          can be expressed as x||x where x is a 8 bit number.
6      */
7      uint32_t v,v1,i,dif,t1,t2,t3;
8      int count=0,z;
9          /* note that here z is a signed integer, and all the
10     other variables used are unsigned integers*/
11     //v cannot be 0 or x7FFFFFFF as then one of v or v' would be
          0.
12     for(v=1;v<0x7FFFFFFF;v++)
13     {
14         v1=v^0x7FFFFFFF;
15         if(v>=v1)
16             dif=v-v1;
17         else
18         {
19             z=v-v1+0x7FFFFFFF;
20             dif=z;
21         }
22     //the conditions
23         if((dif & 0x7FFF0000)==0)
24         {
25             if((((dif & 0xFF00)>>8)==(dif & 0xFF))
26             {
27                 printf("v=%x v1=%x dif=%x \n",v,v1,dif);
28                 count++;
29             }
30         }
31     }
32 printf("%d \n",count);
33 return 0;
34 }
```

Code 4.5 Finding candidate v and $\widetilde{v}$

This implementation gives us 255 pairs of $(v, \widetilde{v})$ and since they can be interchanged, the total number of such values will be 510. From the output of the code, we observe that v can be one of the following type:

$$v = \begin{cases} 1_{16} \parallel y \parallel 1 \parallel y, \\ 0 \parallel 1_{15} \parallel y \parallel 0 \parallel y, \\ 1 \parallel 0_{15} \parallel \bar{y} \parallel 1 \parallel \bar{y}, \\ 0_{16} \parallel \bar{y} \parallel 0 \parallel \bar{y}, \text{ where } \bar{y} \neq \mathbf{0}. \end{cases} \qquad (4.12)$$

The point to note is that each of the choice of the pair $(v, \tilde{v})$ uniquely determines the value of Δiv_0.

With these findings demonstrated here, we now explain the attack related to the IV difference in the first byte. The attack first identifies the keys for which there exists IV pair which could generate identical keystreams and the probability of finding such a key is calculated further. We know that initially, $R_1 = R_2 = 0$. Since $w = (X_0 \oplus R_1) + R_2 = X_0$ which implies the following:

$$\begin{aligned} u &= (X_0 \oplus X_3) \gg 1 \\ &= \big((s_{15H} \parallel s_{14L}) \oplus (s_{2L} \parallel s_{0H})\big) \gg 1 \\ &= \big((k_{15} \parallel \text{0x8F} \parallel \text{0x9A} \parallel iv_{14}) \oplus (\text{0x6B} \parallel iv_2 \parallel k_0 \parallel \text{0x89})\big) \gg 1 \\ &= \big((k_{15} \parallel iv_2 \parallel k_0 \parallel iv_{14}) \oplus \text{0x6B8F9A89}\big) \gg 1. \end{aligned}$$

The next observation is that in the computation of u the following bytes $\{k_{15}, iv_2, k_0, iv_{14}\}$ are involved. We have also seen that the computation of v involves s_0, s_4, s_{10}, s_{13} and s_{15}. Therefore in total 7 bytes of IV, $\{iv_0, iv_2, iv_4, iv_{10}, iv_{13}, iv_{14}, iv_{15}\}$ and 5 bytes of key, $\{k_0, k_4, k_{10}, k_{13}, k_{15}\}$ are involved in the computation of both v and u. Hence, the total search space becomes $2^{8 \times 12} = 2^{96}$.

This search space is further reduced by intelligent manipulations derived from the forms of v that we have already described in Eq. (4.12). Four groups of solutions are found, which satisfy all the constraints. Each group corresponds to one of the four forms that v is found to acquire. We show the calculation for one of the cases and directly put up the results for the other three cases.

$$u = v = (1_{16} \parallel y \parallel 1 \parallel y)$$

We know that u is also equal to $\big((k_{15} \parallel iv_2 \parallel k_0 \parallel iv_{14}) \oplus \text{0x6B8F9A89}\big) \gg 1$. Equating the most significant 15 bits, we get

$$((k_{15} \parallel iv_2) \oplus \text{0x6B8F}) \gg 1 = 1_{15}.$$

From that we derive that $k_{15} \oplus \text{0x6B} = \text{0xFF}$. That is, $k_{15} = \text{0x94}$. Similarly, we get that $iv_2 = \text{0x70}$ and $k_0 = \text{0x9A} \oplus (y\|1)$. All 8 bits of iv_{14} cannot be decided from the constraints as we get $iv_{14} \gg 1 = \text{0x44} \oplus y$. We write down the four groups of solution below.

$$\text{Group 1}: \begin{cases} u = v = (1_{16} \parallel y \parallel 1 \parallel y) \\ k_{15} = 0\text{x}94 \\ iv_2 = 0\text{x}70 \\ k_0 = 0\text{x}9A \oplus (y \parallel 1) \\ iv_{14} \gg 1 = 0\text{x}44 \oplus y \end{cases} \qquad \text{Group 2}: \begin{cases} u = v = (0 \parallel 1_{15} \parallel y \parallel 0 \parallel y) \\ k_{15} = 0\text{x}14 \\ iv_2 = 0\text{x}70 \\ k_0 = 0\text{x}9A \oplus (y \parallel 0) \\ iv_{14} \gg 1 = 0\text{x}44 \oplus y \end{cases}$$

$$\text{Group 3}: \begin{cases} u = v = (0_{15} \parallel \bar{y} \parallel 0 \parallel \bar{y}) \\ k_{15} = 0\text{x}6B \\ iv_2 = 0\text{x}8F \\ k_0 = 0\text{x}9A \oplus (\bar{y} \parallel 0) \\ iv_{14} \gg 1 = 0\text{x}BB \oplus \bar{y} \end{cases} \qquad \text{Group 4}: \begin{cases} u = v = (1 \parallel 0_{15} \parallel \bar{y} \parallel 1 \parallel \bar{y}) \\ k_{15} = 0\text{x}EB \\ iv_2 = 0\text{x}8F \\ k_0 = 0\text{x}9A \oplus (\bar{y} \parallel 1) \\ iv_{14} \gg 1 = 0\text{x}BB \oplus \bar{y} \end{cases}$$

Now we look at the other three key bytes taking part in the state update process, namely $k_{13}, k_{10},$ and k_4 and the IV bytes, which are iv_{15}, iv_{13}, iv_4 and iv_{10}. We can write the computation of newly generated state word as follows:

$$v = 2^{15}s_{15} + 2^{17}s_{13} + 2^{21}s_{10} + 2^{20}s_4 + (1 + 2^8)s_0 \mod (2^{31} - 1) \qquad (4.13)$$

Now, $s_i = k_i \parallel d_i \parallel iv_i$ and, Therefore, $s_i = k_i 2^{15} + d_i 2^8 + iv_i$. Substituting this in (4.13) and also substituting the values of the constants, we get

$$\begin{aligned} v &= (1 + 2^{23})k_0 + 2^7 k^{15} + 2^9(k_{13} + 2^3 k_4 + 2^4 k_{10}) + (1 + 2^8)iv_0 \\ &\quad + 2^{15}(iv^{15} + 2^2 iv_{13} + 2^5 iv_4 + 2^6 iv_{10}) + 0\text{x}451\text{BFe1B} \mod (2^{31} - 1) \end{aligned}$$

Now we define $k_{13} + 2^3 k_4 + 2^4 k_{10}$ to be $sum1$ and $iv_{15} + 2^2 iv_{13} + 2^5 iv_4 + 2^6 iv_{10}$ to be $sum2$. The maximum value of sum1 and sum2 are 6375 and 25755 respectively. With these conditions in place and using the four groups of solutions, an algorithm is formed that detects the weak keys. The C-code of that algorithm is provided in Code 4.6.

```
1  #define all1 0x7FFFFFFF
2  uint32_MAC AddM(uint32_MAC a,uint32_MAC b)
3  {
4      uint32_MAC c = a + b;
5      return (c & all1) + (c >> 31);
6  }
7  #define MulByPow2(x, k) (((((x) << k) | ((x) >> (31 - k)))) & all1
    )
8  #define DivByPow2(x, k) (((((x) >> k) | ((x) << (31 - k)))) & all1
    )
9  int main()
10 {
11     int y,sum1,iv0,iv2,k0,k15,t1,t2=0,ks,v,v1,v2,u,st1,sum2,
12     defv,defiv0,iv0new,count=0,iv14,ch;
13
```

```
14      for(ch=1;ch<=4;ch++)
15      {
16          for(y=0;y<128;y++)
17          {
18              // Group 1.
19              if(ch==1)
20              {
21                      iv14=y^0x44;k15=0x94;iv2=0x70;k0=0x9A^((y<<1)|1)
;
22                      u=0x7fff8000+0x80+y+(y<<8);
23              }
24              //Group 2.
25              if(ch==2)
26              {
27                      k15=0x14;iv2=0x70;k0=0x9A^((y<<1)|0);iv14=y^0x44
;
28                      u=0x3fff8000+y+(y<<8);
29              }
30              //Group 3.
31              if(ch==3)
32              {
33                      k15=0x6b;iv2=0x8f;k0=0x9a^((y^0x7f)<<1);
34                      iv14=0xbb^(y^0x7f);u=((y^0x7f)<<8)+(y^0x7f);
35              }
36              //Group 4.
37              if(ch==4)
38              {
39                      k15=0xeb;iv2=0x8f;k0=0x9a^(((y^0x7f)<<1)|1);
40                      iv14=0xbb^(y^0x7f);u=0x40000080+((y^0x7f)<<8)+(y
^0x7f);
41              }
42
43              if(u!=0 && u!=0x7fffffff)
44              {
45                  for(sum1=0;sum1<=6375;sum1++)
46                  {
47                      for(iv0=0;iv0<=255;iv0++)
48                      {
49                          t2=0;
50                          t1=MulByPow2(k15,7);
51                          t2=AddM(t1,t2);
52                          t1=MulByPow2(k0,23);
53                          t2=AddM(t1,t2);
54                          t2=AddM(t2,k0);
55                          t1=MulByPow2(sum1,9);
56                          ks=AddM(t1,t2);
57                          v1=MulByPow2(iv0,8);
58                          v2=AddM(v1,iv0);
59                          st1=u-ks;
60                          if(st1<=0)
61                              st1+=0x7FFFFFFF;
62                          st1-=v2;
63                          if(st1<=0)
64                              st1+=0x7FFFFFFF;
65                          st1-=0x451bfe1b;
66                          if(st1<=0)
67                              st1+=0x7FFFFFFF;
68                          sum2=DivByPow2(st1,15);
```

```
69
70                              if(sum2<25756)
71                              {
72                                      v=u;
73                                      v1=u^0x7FFFFFFF;
74
75                                      defv=v-v1;
76                                      if(defv<=0)
77                                              defv+=0x7FFFFFFF;
78
79                                      if((defv%0x101)==0)
80                                      {
81                                              defiv0=defv/0x101;
82                                              iv0new=iv0-defiv0;
83                                              count++;
84                                      }
85                                      else
86                                      {
87                                              defv=v1-v;
88                                              if(defv<=0)
89                                                      defv+=0x7FFFFFFF;
90                                              defiv0=defv/0x101;
91                                              iv0new=iv0+defiv0;
92                                              count++;
93                                      }
94                              }
95                      }
96              }
97      }
98 }
99 }
100 printf("count=%d",count);
101 return 0;
102 }
```

Code 4.6 Finding weak keys

In this code, we find out the candidate weak keys. It is to be noted that only 5 bytes of keys are determined via this algorithm, and the other bytes of the key does not impact the security measure in terms of this attack. We get a total of 9934 solutions. Each solution is a tuple of $(k_{15}, k_0, sum1, sum2, iv_0^{(1)}, iv_0^{(2)}, iv_2, iv_{14})$ that result in identical keystreams. Since the value of $sum1$ is bounded by 0 and 6376 and it can be viewed as a function $f_{sum1} : f_{sum1}(k_{13}, k_{10}, k_4) = sum1$. Therefore, $f_{sum1} : s^{24} \to 6376$ and each value of sum represents on average $\frac{2^{24}}{6376}$ choice of k_{13}, k_{10}, k_4. Therefore, the total number of $(k_{15}, k_{13}, k_{10}, k_4, k_0)$ tuples are $\frac{2^{24}}{6376} \times 9934 \approx 2^{24.7}$ Since the total possible such tuples is 2^{40}, we can say a random key is weak with probability $\frac{2^{24.7}}{2^{40}} \approx 2^{-15}$.

The complete procedure of the attack is as follows.

1. First decide if a key is weak, by using each of the 9934 tuples of $(sum2, iv_0^{(1)}, iv_0^{(2)})$. This can be done as the equation $sum2 = iv_{15} + 2^2 iv_{13} + 2^5 iv_4 + 2^6 iv_{10}$ has at least one solution for any value of $sum2$.

2. If the key is weak, it will produce an identical keystream for any one of the chosen IV tuples. If the key is weak, we will be able to find the 5 key bytes with less than 2^{40} complexity.

If for any IV_1 and IV_2 choice, the key produces identical key streams, then that definitely gives us the value of k_0, k_{15} and $sum1$. Now depending on the value of $sum1$, we can find out the other 3 key bytes with maximum $\frac{2^{24}}{9934}$ checks, which is approximately $2^{11.5}$. In the best cases, this time taken can even be 1, if $sum1 = 0$, that means all the three key bytes are 0. The other 11 key bytes need to be searched exhaustively, and therefore the algorithm finds the complete key with $2^{88+11.5} \approx 2^{100}$ worst-case time complexity.

4.2.2 Difference in the Second Byte of IV

Another attack was described which dealt with cases where the IV difference is in the second byte. The methodology is quite similar to the case we have explained and, therefore, we omit it for redundancy. The major difference in this case is that the registers of the nonlinear function are not 0 anymore, as the difference is flushed after two clockings and by then the registers have been clocked once according to the LFSR procedure. This results in different calculations and more key and IV bytes are involved. Therefore, the complexity of the attack and the probability of success are both changed. In fact, in this attack, every key is weak, as there is an IV pair for every key which results in identical key streams. The complexity of this attack is 2^{67}. The main weakness exploited in this case was that u was XOR'ed with v. The current version ZUC 1.6 was formed after correcting these weaknesses as we have seen in Sect. 3.3 of Chap. 3.

In Appendix A, we have provided instances of key, IV pairs for both the different locations (i.e., in the first and second bytes).

4.3 Forgery Attack on EIA-128

A forgery attack on EIA-128 was proposed by Fuhr et al. (2010). In the integrity protocol, every message is verified by a 32 bit MAC which is generated using an integrity key IK and an initialization vector IV mutually decided between the mobile equipment device and the transceiver station. A forgery attack essentially intends to create a MAC for a message so that it would be accepted by the protocol without the adversary knowing the integrity key. This attack exploited the weakness in the one time mask of the protocol. The model of the attack is as follows. Suppose an adversary knows the MAC corresponding to a particular message M for an unknown IK and known IV. Given this information, the attacker could generate the MAC for a related message $\tilde{M}$ with high probability. This attack did not point to a weakness in the structure and working of ZUC itself, but on the EIA protocol that used ZUC as a component. This weakness was then corrected in the later versions prior to its inclusion in the LTE standard. We now explain the attack technically and discuss the reason behind the weakness. Further, we explain how this weakness is mitigated in the later version.

4.3.1 Methodology of the Forgery Attack

We first look into the working principle of the EIA protocol on which the forgery attack was performed by Fuhr et al. (2010). The description of that EIA protocol is described in Algorithm 4.3.

Algorithm 4.3: Old Version of EIA Protocol.

1 **Input:** $IK \in \{0, 1\}^k$, $IV \in \{0, 1\}^n$, $M = (m_0, m_1, \ldots, m_{l-1}) \in \{0, 1\}^l$;
2 **Output:** MAC;
3 $(x_0, x_1, \ldots, x_{l+63}) \leftarrow S(IK, IV)_{|l+63}$;
4 $\quad\quad\quad\quad\quad\quad$ ▷ S is the output of ZUC when initialized with IK and IV ;
5 **for** $i = 0$ *to* $l - 1$ **do**
6 $\quad$ $W_i \leftarrow (x_i, x_{i+1}, \ldots, x_{i+31})$;
7 $\quad$ **if** $m_i = 1$ **then**
8 $\quad\quad$ | $MAC \leftarrow MAC \oplus W_i$;
9 $\quad$ **end**
10 **end**
11 $W_l \leftarrow (x_l, x_{l+1}, \ldots, x_{l+31})$;
12 $MAC \leftarrow MAC \oplus W_l$ $\quad\quad\quad\quad$ ▷ This is added independent of M ;
13 $W_{mask} \leftarrow (x_{l+32}, x_{l+33}, \ldots, x_{l+63})$;
14 $MAC \leftarrow MAC \oplus W_{mask}$;
15 **return** MAC;

From the Algorithm 4.3, it can be observed that

$$MAC = \bigoplus_{i=0}^{l-1} m_i' W_i \oplus W_l \oplus W_{mask}'.$$

In this algorithm, a sliding window protocol is applied to take 32 consecutive keystream bits at every round, which is then XOR'ed with the accumulator (the MAC variable). Depending on the value of one message bit at every round, as we have already discussed in Chap. 3. At last, two 32-bit words W_l and W_{mask} are taken and XOR'ed with the accumulator. These last two words are two disjoint 32-bit words taken out of the keystream.

The weakness of the protocol lies in the fact that the one time mask W_{mask}, which does not have any keystream bit in common with any of the W_i's, is chosen as the next 32 bits of the keystream. Suppose $M_1 = (m_0, m_1, \ldots, m_{l-1})$ and $M_2 = (0, m_0, m_1, \ldots, m_{l-1})$ two messages. It can be easily seen that if for a given key and IV, the MAC generated for M_1 is MAC_1, then for M_2 the MAC value MAC_2 will be $(MAC_1 \ll 1, \beta)$ where β is a single bit. This argument is proven in Eq. (4.14).

$$
\begin{aligned}
MAC_2 &= \bigoplus_{i=0}^{l} m_i' W_i \oplus W_{l+1} \oplus W_{mask}' \\
&= \bigoplus_{i=0}^{l-1} m_i W_{i+1} \oplus W_{l+1} \oplus W_{mask}' \\
&= \bigoplus_{i=0}^{l-1} m_i (W_i \ll 1, b_{i+32}) \oplus (W_l \ll, b_{l+32}) \oplus (W_{mask} \ll 1, b_{l+64}) \\
&= \left(\left(\left(\bigoplus_{i=0}^{l-1} m_i W_i \right) \oplus W_l \oplus W_{mask} \right) \ll 1, \beta \right) \\
&= (MAC_1 \ll 1, \beta)
\end{aligned}
\tag{4.14}
$$

This bit β can be guessed correctly with a probability of $\frac{1}{2}$ and therefore the adversary can forge the MAC for M_2 if (s)he knows the MAC for M_1 for a given key and IV. This weakness was mitigated in the later version of protocol. Now we describe the updated algorithm which is used to generate the MAC value. After that we explain how the weakness is mitigated.

Algorithm 4.4: Updated EIA Protocol (Specification of the 3GPP Confidentiality and Integrity Algorithms 128-EEA3 and 128-EIA3 2011b)

1 **Input:** $IK \in \{0, 1\}^k$, $IV \in \{0, 1\}^n$, $M = (m_0, m_1, \ldots, m_{l-1}) \in \{0, 1\}^l$;
2 **Output:** MAC $(x_0, x_1, \ldots, x_{l+63}) \leftarrow S(IK, IV)_{|l+63}$;
3 $l1 \leftarrow \lceil \frac{l}{32} \rceil + 32$;
4   ▷ S is the output of ZUC when initialized with IK and IV. ;
5 **for** $i = 0$ *to* $l - 1$ **do**
6 $\quad$ $W_i \leftarrow x_i, x_{i+1}, \ldots, x_{i+31}$;
7 $\quad$ **if** $m_i = 1$ **then**
8 $\quad\quad$ $MAC \leftarrow MAC \oplus W_i$;
9 $\quad$ **end**
10 **end**
11 $W_l \leftarrow (x_l, x_{l+1}, \ldots, x_{l+31})$;
12 $MAC \leftarrow MAC \oplus W_l$ ▷ This is added independent of M ;
13 $W_{mask} \leftarrow x_{32(l-1)}, x_{32(l-1)+1}, \ldots, x_{32(l-1)+31}$;
14 $MAC \leftarrow MAC \oplus W_{mask}$;
15 **return** MAC;

The Algorithm 4.4 is almost identical to the Algorithm 4.3 which had the weakness. The only difference is that in the first protocol, the $(l + 32)$ to $(l + 63)$th bits were taken as the one time mask, but in this case of Algorithm 4.4, a new, different output word of ZUC is taken. This change makes the previous attack infeasible. In the case of Algorithm 4.3, we obtained

$$MAC_2 = \left(\left(\left(\bigoplus_{i=0}^{l-1} m_i W_i \right) \oplus W_l \oplus W_{mask} \right) \ll 1, \beta \right)$$
$$= (MAC_1 \ll 1, \beta) \tag{4.15}$$

But in the case of corrected protocol (Algorithm 4.4), the assignment would be

$$MAC_2 = \left(\left(\left(\bigoplus_{i=0}^{l-1} m_i W_i \right) \oplus W_l \right) \ll 1, \beta \right) \oplus W'_{mask}.$$

Now, if $l \neq l'$ then W_{mask} and W'_{mask} are unrelated, and thus the relation described in Eq. (4.15) cannot be obtained.

If, $l = l'$, then $W_{mask} = W'_{mask}$. Hence, $MAC_1 = MAC_2$ implies $\bigoplus_{i=0}^{l} m'_i W_i \oplus W_{l+1} = \bigoplus_{i=0}^{l-1} m_i W_i \oplus W_l$ or, $H(M, K, IV) = H(M', K, IV)$. The probability of such occurrence is $\frac{1}{2^{32}}$ due to the uniform distribution property of H.

References

Fuhr T, Gilbert H, Reinhard J, Videau M (2010) A forgery attack on the candidate LTE integrity algorithm 128-EIA3 (updated version). Citeseer

Specification of the 3GPP Confidentiality and Integrity Algorithms 128-EEA3 and 128-EIA3. Document 4: Design and Evaluation Report. Date: 9th September (2011b). https://www.gsma.com/security/wp-content/uploads/2019/05/EEA3_EIA3_Design_Evaluation_v2_0.doc

Specification of the 3GPP Confidentiality and Integrity Algorithms 128-EEA3 and 128-EIA3. ETSI/SAGE, Document 2: ZUC Specification, Version 1.6, 28th June (2011a). https://www.gsma.com/aboutus/wp-content/uploads/2014/12/eea3eia3zucv16.pdf

Wu H, Huang T, Ha Nguyen P, Wang H, Ling S (2012) Differential attacks against stream cipher ZUC. In: International conference on the theory and application of cryptology and information security (Asiacrypt 2012). Springer, Berlin, pp 262–277

Chapter 5
Concluding Remarks

In this effort, we present a comprehensive document on the ZUC stream cipher. ZUC is used in one of the security standards of the LTE architecture (4G) and the New Radio Architecture (5G) of mobile telephony, among many of its applications worldwide (primarily in China).

In the Chap. 1, we have laid down the mathematical and cryptographic framework to understand the details of this cipher. We began with some basic ideas related to cryptology and then proceeded toward an explanation of the symmetric key cryptosystems, and more specifically stream ciphers. Next, the concepts of finite fields are discussed. Understanding the concept of finite fields is necessary to understand different constructions of stream ciphers. In fact, the design of ZUC is based on Linear Feedback Shift Register (LFSR) over a finite field. We also describe the idea of LFSRs in details, their properties and how LFSRs are defined over a finite field. Then we concentrate on Boolean functions and their various cryptographic properties. The security of ZUC is related to the robustness of the two substitution boxes (S-boxes) used in the cipher. As we have discussed in detail, S-boxes are in fact vector (multiple outputs) Boolean functions. Therefore, understanding the cryptographic properties of Boolean functions is essential in this regard. We also provide certain background to explain where exactly the ZUC cipher is placed in the third-generation partnership project (3GPP).

The second chapter is mostly a description of several protocols related to security in mobile communication network. The security protocols, namely the authentication, integrity and confidentiality algorithms used in the different generations of mobile telephony are discussed in brief. An overview of the security provided in different phases of voice and data transmission in telephony is also provided.

The third chapter describes the working principle of the cipher in complete detail. The chapter starts by describing the different components of the cipher, namely the LFSR, the Bit Reorganization layer and the Nonlinear function (F). Although these components are explained and the security provided by them has been analyzed, there are many questions and problems that require further analysis and research. The first component described in the cipher is the LFSR. As discussed, the LFSR is

C. S. Mukherjee et al., *Design and Cryptanalysis of ZUC*,
SpringerBriefs on Cyber Security Systems and Networks,
https://doi.org/10.1007/978-981-33-4882-0_5

built on $GF(2^{31} - 1)$, and in every state word, the value 0 is replaced by $2^{31} - 1$. The natural question that arises from this choice is as follows.

Research Problem 5.1   How does the structure of the LFSR affect the overall security and randomness of the cipher? One should note that the probability of a bit being 0 or 1 is not same in any of the 32-bit registers used in the Bit Reorganization Layer. Can this bias (though very small) in the Bit Reorganization Layer lead to an adversary in observing some non-randomness?   □

Further to the analysis of the Bit Reorganization layer, the nonlinear functions should also be studied carefully. The S-boxes used in the function are of particular interest as their cryptographic properties are related to the security parameters. One of the S-Boxes (denoted by S_1) used is an affine transformation of the S-Box used in AES and the other one (denoted by S_0) is designed from scratch for the purpose of being used in ZUC. The two S-boxes have different cryptographic properties, such as nonlinearity and differential uniformity, with S_1 being more robust on the basis of each of these properties. This leads to the next question.

Research Problem 5.2   Will the cryptographic properties of ZUC would have been better if an affine transformation of S_1, or an S-Box having comparable parameters as S_1 had been used in place of S_0?   □

We are also aware of the importance of efficient implementation of ciphers used in telephony. One may refer to Avanzi and Brumley (2013) for an efficient implementation of ZUC in software. Further, lightweight implementation with the lowest possible number of gates is also an interesting problem both theoretically and from the application point of view. In this line, there are several efficient implementations of the S-boxes used in AES (see Maximov and Ekdahl 2019 and references therein). Thus, it is important to implement S_0 with minimum possible gates.

Research Problem 5.3   Does there exist a more efficient implementation of the S-box S_0 than the ones that are currently in use?   □

The ZUC cipher being a component of a standard, the components of the design, its working principle, pseudo-code and working c-code are available. These we have discussed in Chap. 3. There is no serious attack on the final version of the cipher, that is ZUC 1.6. However, there are several weaknesses known in the earlier versions, such as ZUC 1.4. These cryptanalytic results are explained in Chap. 4. The differential attack on ZUC 1.4 exploited some weaknesses in the initialization mode. There were also serious cryptanalytic observations on the integrity algorithm in the earlier version.

   In the last section of Chap. 3, we present the description of ZUC-256. Note that this is not a part of any standard yet. However, the latest telephony architecture, New Radio (5G) has the provision for upgrading to 256-bit security, where the session key used is 256-bit in size. One important reason for this is the issues related to quantum adversary that can effectively reduce the secret key size by an order of two using Grover's algorithm (Grover 1996). The issue of quantum adversary is much more devastating against factorization and discrete logarithm-based public key cryptosystems as evident from Shor's quantum factorization algorithm (Shor 1994), but that is not in the scope of this book.

As we have already discussed, this version is called ZUC-256 and differs from the 128-bit version only in the key loading process. This part, in particular, has a lot of areas that need to be analyzed so that the cipher is robust in 256-bit mode. as it is currently in its 128-bit mode. There has already been some analysis (Ding et al. 2020) that shows that the security provided by ZUC-256 has already been compromised to 230-bit. Thus, we need to consider the following issues.

Research Problem 5.4 Can the modification in the initialization phase only provide the security in 256-bit scenario? Can we get convinced that the existing state size is enough to guarantee a larger key size? ☐

As we have pointed out, the fourth chapter presents an account of the major cryptanalytic results obtained in relation with the ZUC cipher and the protocols related to it. The first one is a differential attack on ZUC 1.4 that resulted in the initialization phase procedure being changed. We have also discussed that the present version ZUC 1.6 is reversible. This reversibility does not show any additional vulnerability so far.

Finally, one of the important areas related to cryptanalysis that is not very evolved in case of ZUC is side channel and fault attacks. A broad framework of Differential Fault Attack may be referred to Maitra et al. (2017) and the references therein. Such attacks may be exercised on different versions of ZUC. We have also noted the work Ming et al. (2012) that discussed on side channel attacks against ZUC. Side channel attacks and fault attacks are very powerful tools in practical scenario and resistance of ZUC against these kinds of attacks need to rigorously analyzed further.

Research Problem 5.5 Can there be a fault attack on ZUC which reduces the security of the 128-bit or 256-bit version, or both? What are the measures to be considered to make the cipher resistant against various side channel attacks? ☐

As a final comment, we should re-emphasize that a cryptosystem is only as secure as its weakest link. Thus, this book is only a starting point on the analysis of the ZUC stream cipher. We look forward to further analysis in this regard.

References

Avanzi R, Brumley BB (2013) Faster 128-EEA3 and 128-EIA3 software. https://eprint.iacr.org/2013/428.pdf

Ding J, Johansson T, Maximov A (2020) Spectral analysis of ZUC-256. In: IACR transactions on symmetric cryptology, vol 2020, no 1, pp 266–288. https://eprint.iacr.org/2019/1352.pdf

Grover L (1996) A fast quantum mechanical algorithm for database search. In: Proceedings of 28th annual symposium on the theory of computing, pp 212–219. http://xxx.lanl.gov/abs/quant-ph/9605043

Maitra S, Siddhanti A, Sarkar S (2017) A differential fault attack on plantlet. IEEE Trans Comput 66(10):1804–1808

Maximov A, Ekdahl P (2019) New circuit minimization techniques for smaller and faster AES S-boxes. IACR-CHES-2019. https://eprint.iacr.org/2019/802.pdf

Ming T, Ping Pan C, Zhen Long Q (2012) Differential power analysis on ZUC algorithm. https://eprint.iacr.org/2012/299.pdf

Shor PW (1994) Algorithms for quantum computation: discrete logarithms and factoring. In: Proceedings of 35th annual symposium on foundations of computer science, IEEE Press, Los Alamitos, CA

Appendix
Test Vectors for ZUC

Comparison Test Vector 1:

key: 0x7b || 0x95 || 0xc1 || 0x57 || 0x2a || 0x96 || 0x75 || 0x4 || 0xd1 || 0x65
  || 0x55 || 0x39 || 0x2e || 0x75 || 0x31 || 0xf3

IV_1: 0x5c || 0x50 || 0xf1 || 0xa || 0x0 || 0xd9 || 0x2f || 0xe0 || 0x30 || 0xcb
  || 0x0 || 0x2d || 0xcc || 0x0 || 0x0 || 0x11

IV_2: 0x5c || 0xb6 || 0xf1 || 0xa || 0x0 || 0xd9 || 0x2f || 0xe0 || 0x30 || 0xcb
  || 0x0 || 0x2d || 0xcc || 0x0 || 0x0 || 0x11

- -

Keystream for ZUC 1.4:

For (key, IV_1): 0xf09cc17d 0x41f12d3f 0x453ac0c3 0xcadcef9f
  0xf98fb964 0xca6e576e 0xb48b813 0x6c43da22

For (key, IV_2): 0xf09cc17d 0x41f12d3f 0x453ac0c3 0xcadcef9f
  0xf98fb964 0xca6e576e 0xb48b813 0x6c43da22

- -

Keystream for ZUC 1.6:

For (key, IV_1): 0xa8b7747a 0xd94d7317 0x2c390b9b 0xdc8479b9
  0x4bd5d295 0xd15a3b87 0xe2363e7f 0x257ea9be

For (key, IV_2): 0x83412913 0x8f1510ca 0x75e0eb8e 0x37b8dcc7
  0x24b173d7 0x699c68f0 0x547c9e5c 0x6bd297b3

© The Author(s), under exclusive license to Springer Nature Singapore Pte Ltd. 2021
C. S. Mukherjee et al., *Design and Cryptanalysis of ZUC*,
SpringerBriefs on Cyber Security Systems and Networks,
https://doi.org/10.1007/978-981-33-4882-0

Comparison Test Vector 2:

key: 0x57 || 0x4 || 0x5f || 0xd || 0xa1 || 0x20 || 0xc7 || 0x3d || 0x14 || 0x93
‖0x38 ‖ 0x54 ‖ 0x7e ‖ 0xcd ‖ 0xa5 ‖ 0x94

IV_1: 0xa6 ‖ 0xa6 ‖ 0x70 ‖ 0x26 ‖ 0xc0 ‖ 0xd6 ‖ 0x22 ‖ 0xd3 ‖ 0xaa ‖ 0x19
‖0x12 ‖ 0x47 ‖ 0x4 ‖ 0x87 ‖ 0x44 ‖ 0x5

IV_2: 0x74 ‖ 0xa6 ‖ 0x70 ‖ 0x26 ‖ 0xc0 ‖ 0xd6 ‖ 0x22 ‖ 0xd3 ‖ 0xaa ‖ 0x19
‖0x12 ‖ 0x47 ‖ 0x4 ‖ 0x87 ‖ 0x44 ‖ 0x5

- -

Keystream for ZUC 1.4:

For (key, IV_1): 0xbfe800d5 0x360a22b 0x6c4554c8 0x67f00672
              0x2ce94f3f 0xf94d12ba 0x11c382b3 0xcbaf4b31

For (key, IV_2): 0xbfe800d5 0x360a22b 0x6c4554c8 0x67f00672
              0x2ce94f3f 0xf94d12ba 0x11c382b3 0xcbaf4b31

- -

Keystream for ZUC 1.6:

For (key, IV_1): 0xf9e1a720 0x563c2457 0x38c761cf 0xbb1893f2
              0xf9a74899 0x363953e 0xab2fb8b5 0xa0d95f7d

For (key, IV_2): 0x965f5846 0xf8a1ac3d 0xf08e3c78 0x83f0d4c7
              0xcccd7f6b 0xe14e6210 0xc92032d5 0xe7d54f8b

Some Test Vectors for ZUC 1.6:
Test Vector 1:
key: 0x0 || 0x0 || 0x0 || 0x0 || 0x0 || 0x0 || 0x0 || 0x0 || 0x0 || 0x0 || 0x0 || 0x0
|| 0x0 || 0x0 || 0x0 || 0x0||

IV: 0x0 || 0x0 || 0x0 || 0x0 || 0x0 || 0x0 || 0x0 || 0x0 || 0x0 || 0x0 || 0x0 || 0x0
|| 0x0 || 0x0 || 0x0 || 0x0||

Keystream: 0x27bede74 0x18082da 0x87d4e5b6 0x9f18bf66
0x32070e0f 0x39b7b692 0xb4673edc 0x3184a48e
- -
Test Vector 2:
key: 0xff || 0xff || 0xff || 0xff || 0xff || 0xff || 0xff || 0xff || 0xff || 0xff
|| 0xff || 0xff || 0xff || 0xff || 0xff || 0xff||

IV: 0xff || 0xff || 0xff || 0xff || 0xff || 0xff || 0xff || 0xff || 0xff || 0xff
|| 0xff || 0xff || 0xff || 0xff || 0xff || 0xff||

Keystream: 0x657cfa0 0x7096398b 0x734b6cb4 0x883eedf4
0x257a76eb 0x97595208 0xd884adcd 0xb1cbffb8
- -
Test Vector 3:
key: 0xaf || 0x11 || 0x23 || 0x55 || 0xf3 || 0x1 || 0x34 || 0x90 || 0xb7 || 0x28
|| 0x76 || 0x8d || 0xea || 0xff || 0x9 || 0x11||

IV: 0x23 || 0x1b || 0xcd || 0x49 || 0xf0 || 0xac || 0x26 || 0x0 || 0x23 || 0xee
|| 0xb5 || 0x21 || 0x12 || 0x40 || 0xff || 0xdd||

Keystream: 0x6eca50e8 0x5b6ec9c8 0x947f9c9b 0x4f192bd0
0xc285d60d 0x76cc8922 0xbbcf1714 0xb6ad8a87

Index

© The Author(s), under exclusive license to Springer Nature Singapore Pte Ltd. 2021   97
C. S. Mukherjee et al., *Design and Cryptanalysis of ZUC*,
SpringerBriefs on Cyber Security Systems and Networks,
https://doi.org/10.1007/978-981-33-4882-0

Printed in the United States
By Bookmasters